UNIVERSITY OF NORTH CAROLINA AT CHAPEL HILL
DEPARTMENT OF ROMANCE LANGUAGES

NORTH CAROLINA STUDIES
IN THE ROMANCE LANGUAGES AND LITERATURES

Founder: URBAN TIGNER HOLMES
Editor: CAROL L. SHERMAN

Distributed by:

UNIVERSITY OF NORTH CAROLINA PRESS

CHAPEL HILL
North Carolina 27515-2288
U.S.A.

NORTH CAROLINA STUDIES IN THE
ROMANCE LANGUAGES AND LITERATURES
Number 273

TRANSPOSING ART INTO TEXTS
IN FRENCH ROMANTIC LITERATURE

TRANSPOSING ART INTO TEXTS IN FRENCH ROMANTIC LITERATURE

BY
HENRY F. MAJEWSKI

CHAPEL HILL
NORTH CAROLINA STUDIES IN THE ROMANCE
LANGUAGES AND LITERATURES
U.N.C. DEPARTMENT OF ROMANCE LANGUAGES
2002

Library of Congress Cataloging-in-Publication Data

Majewski, Henry F.
    Transposing art into texts in French romantic literature / by Henry F. Majewski.
    p. cm. – (North Carolina studies in the Romance languages and literatures; no. 273).
    Includes bibliographical references.
    ISBN 0-8078-9277-7 (paper : alk. paper).
    1. French literature–19th century–History and criticism. 2. Romanticism–France.
3. Art in literature. I. Title. II. Series.

PQ288.M354 S53 2002
850.9'357–dc21   2002025983

Cover design: Heidi Perov

© 2002. Department of Romance Languages. The University of North Carolina at Chapel Hill.

ISBN 0-8078-9277-7

DEPÓSITO LEGAL: V. 1.954 - 2002

ARTES GRÁFICAS SOLER, S. L. - LA OLIVERETA, 28 - 46018 VALENCIA

TABLE OF CONTENTS

	Page
LIST OF ILLUSTRATIONS	9
ACKNOWLEDGEMENTS	11
INTRODUCTION: ART, EKPHRASIS AND THE MUSEUM	13
CHAPTER 1: PAINTING INTO TEXT: THÉOPHILE GAUTIER'S ARTISTIC SCREEN	21
CHAPTER 2: READING MELANCHOLY: FRENCH ROMANTIC INTERPRETATIONS OF DÜRER'S ENGRAVINGS	44
CHAPTER 3: GEORGE SAND'S AESTHETIC DREAM: ARTISTS AND ARTISANS IN *LES MAÎTRES MOSAÏSTES*	62
CHAPTER 4: PAINTING AS INTERTEXT IN BALZAC'S *LA FILLE AUX YEUX D'OR*	77
CHAPTER 5: THE ART COLLECTION: AUTHENTIC VALUES IN BALZAC'S *LE COUSIN PONS*	92
CONCLUSION: LOUIS BOULANGER, THE PAINTER-POET OF ROMANTICISM–FROM MAZEPPA TO PETRARCH	103
WORKS CITED	108
ILLUSTRATIONS	111

LIST OF ILLUSTRATIONS

1. Louis Boulanger, (cover) "Le Supplice de Mazeppa," 1827. Musée des Beaux-Arts, Rouen. By permission.
2. Francisco de Zurbarán, "The Ecstasy of Saint Francis," 1664. Alte Pinakothek, Munich. By permission.
3. Jean-Baptiste-Camille Corot, "Landscape with Lake and Boatman," 1839. The J. Paul Getty Museum. By permission.
4. Albrecht Dürer, "The Knight, Death and the Devil," Engraving, 1513. The Metropolitan Museum of Art, New York. Harris Brisbane Dick Fund. By permission.
5. Albrecht Dürer, "Melencolia I," Engraving, 1514. The Metropolitan Museum of Art, New York. Fletcher Fund, 1919. By permission.
6. "St. Mark in Ecstasy," 1545. St. Mark's Basilica, Venice. Designed by Titian and executed by the Zuccato workshop.
7. Eugène Delacroix, "Wild Horse" (Cheval sauvage), Lithograph. 1828. The Metropolitan Museum of Art, New York. By permission.
8. Eugène Delacroix, "Horse attacked by a Tiger" (Cheval terrassé par un tigre), Lithograph. 1828. The Metropolitan Museum of Art, New York. Rogers Fund, 1922. By permission.
9. Eugène Delacroix, "La Mort de Sardanapale," 1827. Louvre Museum. By permission.
10. Eugène Delacroix, "Femmes d'Alger dans leur appartement," 1834. Louvre Museum. By permission.
11. Louis Boulanger, "Le Triomphe de Pétrarque," 1836. Private collection.
12. Louis Boulanger, "Victor Hugo," 1832. La Maison de Victor Hugo, Paris. By permission.
13. Louis Boulanger, "George Sand," 1837. Private collection. By permission.
14. Louis Boulanger, "Portrait de Balzac en robe de chambre," 1836. Musée des Beaux-Arts, Tours. By permission.

ACKNOWLEDGEMENTS

THIS project developed from many years devoted to the study of French romantic literature, and a more recent interest in art history and especially interarts comparisons. Discussions with graduate students and undergrads in courses I gave on the subject at Brown University were always an important stimulus to my work. In addition I would like to thank my colleague and friend Pierre St. Amand for helping me to make my chapter titles less pedantic (removing the ubiquitous colon) and more lively (if sometimes close to gallicisms). Susan Clifford, who works with me at the Howard Foundation, has taught me to prepare my manuscripts on the computer, and for that new skill I am very grateful to her. Jennifer Gage, an excellent translator and book editor, assisted me very competently in the final preparation of the manuscript. I would also like to thank my friend and young colleague Gretchen Schultz for her wonderful friendship and support. Finally, I owe a debt of gratitude to my friend of many years and late colleague, Professor Albert Salvan, who was able to read all of my chapters except the last one with his customary critical acumen. His encouragement and kindness were always appreciated.

The following literary journals have generously granted me permission to reprint materials previously published in the form of articles: *Symposium, Nineteenth-Century French Studies* and *Romance Quarterly*.

Introduction

ART, EKPHRASIS, AND THE MUSEUM

IMPORTANT critical studies have recently appeared on the theory and poetics of ekphrasis as well as a series of fascinating works that illustrate relationships between art and literary texts.[1] With the advent of post-modernism, or is it post-post-modernism, it is again acceptable to examine the ways in which one artistic medium influences another or attempts to reproduce elements from a related art. Interdisciplinary studies have encouraged the desire to seek relationships beyond the boundaries of a single work of art. The development of cultural studies has produced valuable examina-

---

[1] In his important study *Ekphrasis: The Illusion of the Natural*, Murray Krieger develops the history of the genre from antiquity to the present but deals only with Diderot in the French tradition. Wendy Steiner's book *The Colors of Rhetoric: Problems in the Relation between Modern Literature and Painting* offers close analysis of major modern examples of interarts relations from a rhetorical and semiotic perspective. W. J. Thomas Mitchell has written a series of influential works on word and image including *Iconology: Image, Text, Ideology*. Nineteenth-century writers in the French tradition were treated by David Scott in *Pictorialist Poetics: Poetry and the Visual Arts in 19th Century France*. See note 2 in Chapter 1, p. 23.

Several books of essays that treat both the practice and theory of interarts relations have recently appeared. *Pictures into Words; Theoretical and Descriptive Approaches to Ekphrasis* was edited by Valerie Robillard and Els Jongeneel. It includes one essay devoted to French romantic literature: "The Ekphrastic Components of Victor Hugo's *Notre Dame de Paris*" by N. Kenaan-Kedar. Volume 6 in the series *European Cultures: Studies in Literature and the Arts* is devoted to essays on ekphrasis and intermediality: *Icons-Texts-Iconotexts*, edited by Peter Wagner. Among the French artists and writers represented are Diderot, Watteau and Fragonard. An essay by Alain Montandon deals with Gautier's prose: "Ecritures de l'image chez Théophile Gautier."

tions of the pivotal role of the museum as an institution in nineteenth and twentieth-century society, and especially as a source for literary inspiration.

One of the most useful and comprehensive of these recent studies is James A. W. Heffernan's *Museum of Words: The Poetics of Ekphrasis from Homer to Ashberry*. He provides a clear working definition of the rhetorical term (3); ekphrasis is quite simply the verbal representation of a visual representation. Heffernan analyzes major examples from the description of Achilles' shield in Homer to romantic and contemporary texts. He enriches this definition with the concept of "notional ekphrasis" developed by the poet and critic John Hollander, author of *Artistic Relations* and other works connecting the arts. This concept refers to verbal representations of imagined works of art, such as the paintings Gautier invents and describes in his early romantic poetry about artists and their creative work.[2]

Heffernan's theory of ekphrasis also includes an interesting gender distinction. He claims that the history of this literary genre is largely a paragonal struggle for dominance by the masculine verb over the feminine image. Keat's famous ode to the Grecian Urn, with its "unravished bride of silence," is a primary example of a poem that gives hardness, permanence and stasis to a fragile, momentary (feminine) scene inscribed in the painted urn.

In my opinion, the French tradition (which Heffernan's study does not include) cannot be adequately described in this manner. From the romantics to the symbolists in nineteenth-century France there is above all a rediscovery of the possible enrichment of all art forms through mutual borrowings and correspondences. This concept will eventually be elaborated by Baudelaire in his annual reviews of the Salons and other essays on art and aesthetics.

Rather than a desire to dominate, this quest for more comprehensive art forms, culminating in Wagner's concept of opera as a total work of art, is an ideal that encouraged the development of interarts relations and cooperation between artists. Berlioz and Delacroix are recognized as the most literary of artists; both com-

---

[2] *Albertus ou l'âme et le péché* (1831) and *La Comédie de la mort* (1838) present painters as protagonists of these narrative poems and offer many examples of "transpositions d'art." See Chapter 1, pp. 28-34.

posed music and pictures based on Shakespeare, Byron and Goethe as well as other writers. The poet Gautier, for example, who began his artistic life as a painter, and transposed many visual representations into poems throughout his oeuvre, claimed that language could never equal the expressiveness and subtlety of the visual image. The effort to make poetry more musical and less discursive (e.g. Hugo's *Ballades*), and the use of pictorial techniques such as color symbolism and painterly descriptions in prose (as we will find in Balzac and Sand), are evidence of this cooperative approach to the so-called sister arts.

Gautier's term "transposition d'art," the attempt to transpose elements of one artistic medium into another, is the central concept of this major aspect of the romantic aesthetic whose practice I plan to illustrate and analyze. In the case of Hugo, he is not interested in descriptive representations of paintings, but uses Dürer's engravings to deepen his interpretation of romantic themes and ideas; thus he moves from individual emotion to collective experience of injustice in a poem like "Melancholia." Balzac's admiration for Delacroix is translated into the prose of *La Fille aux yeux d'or* in precise scenes, characters and pictorial language whose meanings are greatly enhanced through reference to specific paintings of the great romantic painter. George Sand employs the mosaic as a stylistic device in her novel *Les Maîtres mosaïstes*, but also projects into the lives of Renaissance mosaic makers her modern, socialist ideals of a community of artists, creating together to accomplish a spiritual goal.

Heffernan introduces another essential aspect of interarts relations with his emphasis on the growth of the modern museum as a cultural institution. He claims that the practice of ekphrasis greatly increased in the modern period due to easier access to famous works of art. He points out, for example, that the arrival of the Elgin marbles in the British Museum undoubtedly influenced Keats and Shelley in their poetry based on visual images of antiquity.[3] Gautier was extraordinarily moved by the Spanish paintings he viewed in Louis Philippe's collection in the Louvre; his volume of verse entitled *España*, including poems about Spanish painters and

---

[3] See Heffernan's chapter on "Romantic Ekphrasis," 94-134.

painting, resulted from this experience as much as from his trip to Spain.

An excellent recent study of the museum, *Museum Memories, History, Technology, Art* by Didier Maleuvre, examines both the positive and negative roles this institution has assumed in modern times. Seen by many philosophers and artists as the protector of the arts, it has also been decried as a force for alienation; the work of art has been removed from the social context in which it served a living function to be isolated and die. The Elgin marbles are again a controversial and ambivalent case in point.

The argument about the role of the museum is very pertinent to my proposal and can provide a meaningful frame to my examination of ekphrastic practice. The Louvre Museum was created in 1793 as a Revolutionary act to preserve and celebrate the nation's artistic heritage; it also became a central depository for Napoleon's spoils detached from their original context. The Louvre certainly made the viewing of great works of art more accessible to a wider audience. Engravings, as well as copies and prints of paintings, had been the best source for knowledge of Western masterpieces before the development of the museum as a state institution.

Balzac's many novels about artists and art in the *Comédie humaine* can provide an important perspective on the function of the museum in post-revolutionary France. Didier Maleuvre devotes a long concluding chapter of his cultural study of museums to Balzac and specifically to *La Peau de chagrin* ("Balzacana," 191-280). Written in 1831, it is one of the first and most important of the *Etudes philosophiques*; it offers an early presentation of Balzac's theory of desire and human will through a modern variation of the Faust myth.

It is in the famous antique shop near the Quai Voltaire that Raphaël de Valentin is offered the talisman, which will permit him to live his desires, and ultimately exhaust his given fund of energy. Maleuvre treats this gallery of the shop as if it were a museum, and, in effect, it is an immense repository for a wide variety of the artifacts and arts of Western civilization. In keeping with the new society of emerging capitalism, every item has been turned into a saleable commodity under the mysterious gaze of the Mephistophelean proprietor. After a long ekphrastic description of a painting of the head of Christ by the Renaissance master, Raphael,

INTRODUCTION: ART, EKPHRASIS, AND THE MUSEUM   17

Balzac quotes the shop's owner: "j'ai couvert cette toile de pièces d'or, dit froidement le marchand" (6: 439). This gallery-museum is, then, for the narrator and Balzac a vast and chaotic storage house for the lifeless remains of Western civilization; the masterworks and artifacts are not valued for their spiritual and aesthetic beauty, or individual worth, but simply as material objects for sale. For Balzac the conservative thinker, this museum symbolizes the disastrous results of the Revolution's destruction of aristocratic patronage of the arts, and the dispersal of goods and fortunes in its aftermath by the emerging, dominant bourgeoisie.

At the other end of Balzac's production is another text in which the museum functions as a primary character. His final novel *Le Cousin Pons* (1847) posits a private museum as an alternative to the questionable authority of a state institution or the thoughtless consumption of art by the avaricious new middle class. In this novel, to be analyzed in detail in the final chapter, the paintings of Pons' collection represent the authentic, essential values of Western civilization. In a curiously optimistic conclusion to this most pessimistic study of human greed, the collection of masterworks will be preserved for posterity almost intact by a rich patron of the arts, a kind of nineteenth-century Getty.

During Raphaël de Valentin's visit to the antique shop he is given the opportunity by the devilish merchant to view the portrait of Christ by his famous namesake, the painter Raphael. He who had seriously contemplated suicide is profoundly moved by this experience which momentarily restores in him the desire to live:

> Quelque parfum épanché des cieux dissipa les tortures infernales qui lui brûlaient la moelle des os. La tête du Sauveur des hommes paraissait sortir des ténèbres figurées par un fond noir; une auréole de rayons étincelait vivement autour de sa chevelure d'où cette lumière voulait sortir; sous le front, sous les chairs, il y avait une éloquente conviction qui s'échappait de chaque trait par de pénétrantes effluves. Les lèvres vermeilles venaient de faire entendre la parole de vie, et le spectateur en cherchaient le retentissement sacré dans les airs [...]. L'Evangile était traduit par la simplicité calme de ces adorables yeux où se réfugiaient les âmes troublées. Enfin la religion catholique se lisait tout entière en un suave et magnifique sourire [...]. Cette peinture inspirait une prière, [...] réveillait toutes les vertus endormies.

> Partageant le privilège des enchantements de la musique, l'oeuvre de Raphael vous jetait sous le charme impérieux des souvenirs, et son triomphe était complet, on oubliait le peintre. Le prestige de sa lumière agissait encore sur cette merveille: par moments, il semblait que la tête s'agitât dans le lointain, au sein de quelque nuage. (6:439)

In this early text Balzac offers a rich and complex example of his use of painting to be found throughout *La Comédie humaine*, and suggests the importance of the function of ekphrastic description for the novelist. The narrator presents the painting with attention to its forms and colors; the shadows behind the Savior's head are figured by a black background which contrasts with the brilliant halo that seems to come forth from his hair and his vermilion lips. The narrator immediately develops the spectator's impressions and reactions to the painting, and then generalizes about the spiritual value of the work.

The painting seems to resonate with religious feeling, "le retentissement sacré dans les airs," and becomes a living symbol of Christ's word, "traduit par la simplicité calme de ses adorables yeux." Balzac moves from the protagonist's reactions to include the reader (vous) in a final apotheosis of the transforming power of art. The painting awakens the love of virtue, and like the enchantment of music, has the ability to place us in the world of past time and memories until we forget the painter himself. The prestige of the painting's light creates the vivid impression that the Christ figure is alive. The reader is startled to recall that this is the same painting previously covered over with money by the antique shop's owner.

Balzac's description attempts to reveal the essence of the work, its magic-like power to restore spiritual need in the spectator. This is perhaps the most important function of ekphrasis for the French romantics: to give permanent verbal form to the more fragile image which is always menaced by destruction in time, and in so doing to reveal its deepest significance. The painting of Christ by itself can indeed represent the essential values of Western spiritual life, but it is now covered with "pièces d'or," hidden by the materialism of contemporary society.

In *La Peau de chagrin* (1831) as well as *Le Cousin Pons* (1847), the "museum" thus contains the art works representing the authentic values of a society that wants to turn them into commodities. At the beginning and end of his career as a writer, Balzac used a verbal representation to preserve and reveal the spiritual meanings of the visual image or work of art, threatened by society's materialism. In this sense only does the verbal dominate the visual, just as Balzac thought that in his novels of the human comedy he could capture and give form to the essential principles, laws and philosophy of his changing society.

The chapters of my study are not limited to the strict examination of ekphrasis or "transposition d'art" in the texts chosen. The romantic writers also developed a sophisticated pictorial language in prose and poetry; they made extensive use of color symbolism and attempted to borrow structural forms from art in their descriptions of décor and landscape, often without reference to a specific painting. As a general rule, in order to avoid undue speculation, I have concentrated on the function of art in romantic poems and prose texts that deal only with clearly identifiable works. Other books could indeed be written about the romantics' essays about art as well as their various theories of aesthetics. I attempt here primarily to illustrate some of the variety and explain the significance of their widespread practice of verbal representation of visual images from the world of art.

CHAPTER 1

PAINTING INTO TEXT: THEOPHILE GAUTIER'S
ARTISTIC SCREEN

THERE has recently been renewed interest in Gautier's numerous writings about the arts, his studies of painters, and his general art criticism. The proceedings of a 1982 colloquium held in Montpellier, *Théophile Gautier, l'Art et l'artiste*, contain excellent essays on many aspects of his aesthetics. Articles deal, for example, with his appreciation of Ingres, his relationship with contemporary landscape artists and the realists, as well as his understanding of Spanish painting.

With the recent publication of David Scott's *Pictorialist Poetics*[1] and Constance Schick's richly detailed study of Gautier's complete poetic production, it seems appropriate to re-examine the precise function of painting in Gautier's verse. Scott's work attempts to define the relationship between poetry and painting from a formalist and semiotic perspective; specific linguistic and prosodic elements are carefully compared to painterly techniques and effects in poets from Bertrand and Gautier to Mallarmé. Schick emphasizes the textual surfaces of Gautier's poetry and makes a convincing case for his modernity. She insists on the complex play of intertextual references in his poems. The expression of a personal "romantic" vision or mimesis of real places and scenes, such as the Spanish landscape, are not only secondary aspects of the poetry, but just poetic signs,

---

[1] Scott studies the role of Gautier as an early exponent of the aesthetics of interarts comparisons, and devotes a chapter to "The Art of Transposition" (88-108). There are two important texts by David Kelley which deal with interarts comparisons: "Gautier et Baudelaire" and "Transpositions."

borrowed or imitated, which contribute to the creation of the poem as autonomous word-game.

My effort here will be to examine one important aspect of the complex intertextual signs informing the poetry. Much has been written about Gautier's poetic device, the "transposition d'art," but there is very little specific analysis of techniques used by the poet to transform pictorial signs into poetic text. I propose, therefore, to study the function of painting in Gautier's poetry as a kind of artistic screen.

The reality of the outside world (landscape, people, past events), as well as the inner world of memory and thought, are frequently transformed by a work of art which stands between the poetic voice and the poem itself. It acts as a filtering device or screen which both projects and reflects reality; it enhances the poet's vision, offering him unusual insight into the significance and value of experience. It is well known that Gautier began his career as a painter and retained his love for painting throughout his life. In fact he often expresses the fundamental inadequacy of language to express the spiritual truths and aesthetic ideals of beauty which the poet is seeking. Primacy is given to painting in his quest, as in "La Diva" of 1838:

> Pourquoi, lassé trop tôt dans une heure de doute,
> Peinture bien-aimée, ai-je quitté ta route?
> Que peuvent tous nos vers pour rendre la beauté,
> Que peuvent de vains mots sans dessin arrêté,
> Et l'épithète creuse et la rime incolore?
> Ah! combien je regrette et combien je déplore
> De ne plus être peintre, en te voyant ainsi
> A Mosé, dans ta loge, O Julia Grisi!
>
> (2: 97, 7-14)

"La Diva" contains many allusions to a long tradition of poetic eulogies of the female form. It presents itself as a paean to the transcendent beauty of the very real Julia Grisi whom the poet wishes to please. In a typical play of ambiguities the poet nevertheless concludes that words that exist without design or color are hollow. They appear as arbitrary signifiers without a real link to reality, and thus are incapable of capturing the essence of her beauty or the poetic ideal. This is precisely the function of painting in Gautier's poetry; it provides a presence to ground the work in reality. It gives his vision of the world an essence in the Derridean sense that it is otherwise lacking. Without painting or other forms of art, especially sculpture in the *Emaux et Camées*, the world is defined by lack and meaninglessness. Art gives it presence, and painting gives his poetry its essence, that is, the possibility of producing significance.

An excellent illustration of this aesthetic concept is found in Gautier's "Le Triomphe de Pétrarque" (1836), which can readily be compared to Hugo's "Fonction du poète" (1839) in *Les Rayons et les ombres* or to Vigny's poems dealing with the artist's role in society.[2] The thematic structure of the poem reveals the poetic speaker's evolution from personal despair to a new confidence in his own creativity: "Il faisait nuit dans moi, nuit sans lune, nuit sombre; / Je marchais en aveugle en tâtant le chemin" (2: 76, 1-2).

Gautier has addressed this poem of the poet's self-discovery to his friend the painter, Louis Boulanger. It is indeed his painting of the poet Petrarch, who is triumphantly acclaimed by an admiring and grateful public, that is at the center of the experience being

---

[2] Alfred de Vigny's contribution to the notion of a meaningful correspondence among the arts has not been examined in great detail. In my chapters on Vigny in *Paradigm and Parody* (19, 157), I discuss two early poems which present interarts comparisons. "Le Déluge" (1823) is an interesting attempt at a "transposition d'art" before similar efforts by Gautier. Vigny transposes into words the pictorial effects and emotions evoked by Girodet's painting of the deluge. In the poem he discusses the almost insurmountable difficulty of the task in view of the complexity of the subject, particularly when he considers the need to suggest the sounds and movement of this cosmic drama. He dreams of a more complete art form in which music, poetry and painting would function together, complementing and reinforcing each other to produce a more expressive, complete art. In "La Beauté idéale" (1824) he expresses his desire for such forms:

> Où donc est la beauté que rêve le poète?
> Aucun d'entre les arts n'est son digne interprète
> Et, souvent il voudrait, par son rêve égaré,
> Confondre ce que Dieu pour l'homme a séparé.
> Il voudrait ajouter les sons à la peinture.
> [...]
> Descends donc, triple lyre, instrument inconnu,
> O toi! Qui parmi nous n'est pas encore venu
> Et qu'en se consumant invoque le génie.
> Sans toi point de beauté, sans toi point d'harmonie:
> Musique, poésie, art pur de Raphael,
> Vous deviendrez un Dieu...mais sur un seul autel. (1: 235)

represented. The sight of the beautiful portrait profoundly moves the discouraged poet:

> Je demeurai longtemps sans pouvoir te parler,
> Plongeant mes yeux ravis au fond de ta peinture
> Qu'un rayon de soleil faisait étinceler.
> (2: 77, 10-12)

He then transposes the painting into poetry, describing it with particular attention to its color scheme, and interprets it by giving voice to the thoughts of the Renaissance poet. The painting thus understood and transposed becomes the point of departure for a representation of the function of poetry as spiritual guidance for humanity. Petrarch painted by Boulanger, transposed by Gautier, becomes the symbol of the "sacred" poet whose idealism and spirituality can illuminate the sense of life for the others.

> Sur l'autel idéal entretenez la flamme,
> Guidez le peuple au bien par le chemin du beau,
> Par l'admiration et l'amour de la femme.
>
> Comme un vase d'albâtre où l'on cache un flambeau,
> Mettez l'idée au fond de la forme sculptée.
> Et d'une lampe ardente éclairez le tombeau.
> (2: 81, 10-15)

Alfred de Vigny's representation of the transformative power of poetry depends on the love of the mysterious Eva in "La Maison du berger"; for Gautier's poet, Boulanger's painting of Petrarch is the agent of change and revelation. Since the picture by Boulanger reveals the spiritual meaning of poetry, it returns to the poet a sense of the universal value of art. At the same time it restores confidence in his own creative talent, and consequently he experiences a kind of rebirth:

> O miracle de l'art! O puissance du beau!
> Je sentais dans mon coeur se redresser mon âme
> Comme au troisième jour le Christ dans son tombeau.
> (2: 78, 9-11)

Painting is therefore the necessary link or protective screen between Gautier's speaker and a disappointing reality. Boulanger's picture becomes the symbol of the spiritual function of art, and leads to the possibility of the speaker's own rebirth as poet.

Gautier in this poem is, of course, contributing to the romantic convention of the "sacre de l'écrivain," which Paul Bénichou has analyzed in fine detail.[3] His conception of the poet in 1836 is idealistic and basically conservative, closer in spirit to Vigny than to Hugo. "L'idée au fond de la forme sculptée" (2: 81, 14) suggests Vigny's concept of the symbol as enthusiasm crystallized in a diamond-hard shape; and Gautier's speaker specifically discourages the artist's participation in rebellion or revolution. He concludes that the dream is preferable to action: "Rêveur harmonieux, tu fais bien de chanter: / C'est là le seul devoir que Dieu donne aux poètes" (2: 80, 22-23).

The collection *Emaux et camées* contains numerous allusions to painters and several "transpositions d'art" whose pictorial sources have been identified with reasonable certainty. Madeleine Cottin in her valuable edition of the text (1968)[4] has provided illustrations of most of the paintings, engravings and statuary represented or suggested. The major emphasis, as is well known, has shifted in this pre-Parnassian poetry to the more resistant, durable forms of art as metaphor for poetry. The final stanza in the last poem entitled "L'Art" advises the poet to:

> Sculpte, lime, cisèle;
> Que ton rêve flottant
> Se scelle
> Dans le bloc résistant!
> (3: 130, 5-8)

The role of painting in these poems is considerably less direct, and fewer descriptions of specific pictures are to be found. The poetic experience is composed of a more general correspondence be-

---

[3] See Bénichou's *Le Sacre de l'écrivain 1750-1830* for a study of the role played by romantic writers in the creation of the concept of the poet-prophet, and writer as spiritual guide.

[4] Among the examples she discusses are "Les Néréides," based on a watercolor by Gendron, and "Etudes de mains," which contains a direct reference to Ingres.

tween the arts that often includes musical reference as well as pictorial ("Symphonie en blanc majeur," "Variations sur le Carnaval de Venise").

Pictorial allusion, nevertheless, is much more prevalent than is usually acknowledged; an entire essay could be devoted to its complex function in Gautier's most famous collection. Since this is generally a more impersonal and seemingly objective poetry, the references to painting are perhaps more subtle and less explicit, and consequently the critic is often tempted to speculate unduly. In the *Emaux et camées* the poet-speaker appears to carry within himself a kind of "musée imaginaire" from which he readily borrows images and figures to create a rich mixture of artistic artifact.

For this reason I prefer to concentrate in this study on the earlier, often neglected volumes of Gautier's poetry in which the artistic screen is identified by the speaker. One example from the *Emaux et camées* can suffice to explain the subtle integration of painting in the text, and exemplify the persistence of its essential role in the poet's creative process.

"Le Château du souvenir" is probably the most personal of the poems in the *Emaux et camées* since its theme is the remembrance of the speaker's past, and especially the people he loved in his youth. In order to reconstruct the time of his happy bohemian life spent with Nerval and the group of the Cénacle, the poet creates the image of a romantic, fantastic castle, which becomes the metaphor of memory and its contents. Cottin suggests that the inspiration for Gautier's description of the abandoned chateau is probably a drawing by Gustave Doré for the *Contes* of Perrault (155). She also thinks that one of the faded tapestries in the memory-castle was inspired by a painting of Chassériau ("Daphné, les hanches dans l'écorce," 1845), that Gautier had admiringly described in *La Presse* the same year (156). There is no textual corroboration, however, for these provocative and credible suggestions of interartistic comparisons. Neither Doré nor Chassériau is cited by Gautier as a source in the poem or elsewhere.

A pictorialist poetic is, indeed, very much active in the poem on both the thematic and textual levels. When the poet-speaker succeeds in reconstructing his "castle of memory" through imagination, and enters the dusty, neglected rooms, he discovers not the people he once knew, but their portraits on the faded wall coverings. The central portion of the poem is then devoted to a representation of these portraits. Painting once again serves as a screen through which to recreate reality, in this case to restore the past. Photography has perhaps assumed a similar function in twentieth-century experience; a literary example would be Breton's novel *Nadja* in which drawings and photographs complement and help to interpret the text.

"Le Château du souvenir" offers a poetic allegory of the speaker's effort to recapture lost time. His difficult voyage to the abandoned castle, its long un-visited rooms, and finally the dusty portraits he discovers symbolize poetry's capacity, like that of painting, to create a reality of its own. For not only does the speaker find the portraits of his former loved ones, but the pictures come to life, and we encounter once again Gautier's paradoxical, personal obsession found throughout his works–the possibility of life in death, and the reality of death in life.[5]

> L'image au sépulcre ravie
> Perd son aspect roide et glacé;
> La chaude pourpre de la vie
> Remonte aux veines du passé.
>
> Les masques blafards se colorent
> Comme au temps où je les connus.
> O vous que mes regrets déplorent,
> Amis, merci d'être venus!
>
> (3: 108, 1-8)

Poetry through painting has the power here to give life to the dead past. In yet another variation of the Pygmalion myth found often in Gautier's stories and poems,[6] the speaker re-animates the portrait of his adored "Cydalise":

> Ma main tremblante enlève un crêpe
> Et je vois mon défunt amour,

---

[5] Examples of this major theme are found in his long poem *La Comédie de la mort* (1838), the novel *Le Roman de la momie* (1857) and the short story "La morte amoureuse" (1836). Marcel Voisin studied the complex imagery of woman and death in *Le Soleil et la nuit: l'imaginaire dans l'oeuvre de T. Gautier*.

[6] See Ross Chambers' article "Gautier et le complexe de Pygmalion."

> Joupons bouffants, taille de guêpe,
> La Cidalise en Pompadour!
>
> (3: 104, 13-16)
>
> [...]
> Elle tressaille à mon approche,
> Et son regard, triste et charmant,
> Sur le mien, d'un air de reproche,
> Se fixe douloureusement.
>
> (3: 104, 25-28)

This "transposition" of the imaginary portrait (Cottin suggests that it is based on a drawing of Camille Rogier [166]) illustrates many of Gautier's pictorialist techniques. The talented beauty called "la Cydalise," celebrated by both Nerval and Gautier, was destined to die young. Gautier captures her ephemeral existence through the evocation of her figure dressed in the faded style of an eighteenth-century Pompadour. He emphasizes colors and the effects of light: her ribboned corsage reveals the pink of her nipples; the lace only half covers the snowy white of her breast with its azure veins. Death is, nevertheless, already present in the humid reflections of light in her eyes; he compares these "moites paillettes" to leaves bitten by an early frost. A reddish tint colors her cheeks but it is just an "éclat trompeur, fard de la mort!"

The poet translates the effect of the sensations produced by the portrait through color imagery and metaphor. He concludes that the Cydalise, whom he loved so briefly, is best remembered as a "gentille morte" (restored to life in his poem), a shadow dressed for a masked ball (who played a minor role in the fantasy world of the Cénacle), and finally a delicately painted flower, a "fleur de pastel"–that is, a painting which poetry revives and perhaps immortalizes.

"Le Château du souvenir" is undoubtedly a rich texture of romantic conventions and already cliché-like images and myths, such as the abandoned castle and the idealized muse. It works effectively, nevertheless, as an allegory of the special role painted images can have in our efforts to restore the past in our lives.

Gautier's most typically romantic works are the long poems *Albertus ou l'âme et le péché* (1831) and *La Comédie de la mort* (1838). Both poems feature painters as protagonists and develop the Faustian theme of the impossible search for the absolute. They contain numerous allusions to paintings and painters and offer several excellent examples of "transposition d'art." They appear as very important transitional works between the seemingly personal, conversational poems resembling the early style of Hugo's *Feuilles d'automne* (1831), and the *Emaux et camées* (1852) based on a pre-Parnassian aesthetic impulse.

Albertus already contains the seeds of Gautier's future artistic philosophy, expressed, however, in exaggerated terms. The protagonist is a Faustian painter, sick with the "mal du siècle." Disillusioned with the limitations of his knowledge, he desires only death. After yet another tragic experience to realize an ideal love, he concludes that the beautiful surfaces of things are perhaps the only recompense for the tragic emptiness of existence.

> Jouissons, faisons-nous un bonheur de surface;
> Un beau masque vaut mieux qu'une vilaine face.
> –Pourquoi l'arracher, pauvres fous?
>
> (1: 163, 72.10-12)

In fact, beautiful surfaces, like the mask, give a presence and can even restore an essence to a corrupt reality devoid of meaning:

> Malheur, malheur à qui dans cette mer profonde
> Du coeur de l'homme jette imprudemment la sonde!
> Car le plomb bien souvent, au lieu de sable d'or,
> De coquilles de nacre aux beaux reflets de moire,
> N'apporte sur le pont que boue infecte et noire.
>
> (1: 163, 72.1-5)

Searching in the depths of the sea, or its analog in the human heart, can reveal the profound corruption of things. It is perhaps preferable to recreate the surface beauty of the silver shells with their silken reflections–and transform them into the enamels and cameos of art. Gautier's rejection of "philosophical" poetry and his espousal of a more concrete, visual art is already clearly projected here.

Albertus worships the painter Raphael (who becomes a protagonist in the following work, *La Comédie de la mort*) because he succeeded in immortalizing ideal beauty. In what might be considered an autobiographical stanza Gautier's poet presents Albertus as a lover of the three sister arts, who if required to choose among them would have aspired to become a new Raphael.

Painting indeed has a major function in the poem. Albertus' atelier is described like Rembrandt's studio, and the Flemish settings of the poem are compared to the paintings of Teniers; many grotesque and fantastic scenes invoke the drawings of Callot and Goya. Color symbolism is constantly used to create atmosphere as well as to symbolize the action. The entire poem, complete with a witches' sabbath and orgy scene, might very well be considered a "transposition d'art." It is an exuberant, even frenetic text in the style of Petrus Borel, a kind of poetic parody of Callot and Goya without precisely identified pictorial sources.

In the center of his atelier Albertus keeps a veiled painting of his dead mistress–Gautier's obsessional figure of "la morte amoureuse," once again. Next to it is his current project, a landscape in the style of Salvator Rosa (1615-1673), the seventeenth-century painter much admired by the young generation, and often referred to by art historians as a proto-romantic.

> Albertus travaillait. – C'était un paysage.
> Salvator eût signé cette toile sauvage.
> Au premier plan des rocs, – au second le donjon
> D'un château dentelant de ses flèches aigües
> Un ciel ensanglanté, semé d'îles de nues.
> Les grands chênes pliaient comme de faibles joncs,
> Les feuilles tournoyaient en l'air; l'herbe flétrie,
> Comme les flots hurlants d'une mer en furie,
> Ondait sous la rafale, et de nombreux éclairs
> De reflets rougeoyants incendiaient les cimes
> Des pins échevelés, penchés sur les abîmes
> Comme sur le puits des enfers.
>
> (1: 167, 81.1-12)

Gautier in a kind of "mise en abîme" is here transposing an imagined painting of his protagonist-painter into poetry through the artistic screen of a Salvatore Rosa landscape as model and reference. This stanza is an excellent illustration of the pictorialist techniques Gautier employed throughout his poetic production. The structure of the painter's landscape is clearly indicated to the reader; the planes from foreground to background–from the rugged, uneven rocks to the dungeon of a chateau under a blood-red sky in the distance–direct the movement of the spectator's gaze. The stormy landscape is dominated by the symbolic red of blood and violence: the sky is "ensanglanté" and lightening inflames the pines with "reflets rougeoyants." The realistic details of the painterly description are, however, transformed and interpreted by the poet's metaphors to suggest the symbolic meaning of the painting and its effect on the viewer-reader: the stormy scene of nature in torment resembles the terrifying entrance to Hell. Romantic personifications–the oaks bend, and the pine trees are frightened–and especially the central comparison between the natural landscape and the ocean evoke the desired response of terror: "Comme les flots hurlants d'une mer en furie" (1: 167, 81.8).

Salvatore Rosa, and presumably Albertus, have successfully recreated the destructive force of nature's storm in their pictures; the verb forms "pliaient," "tournoyaient," "flétrie," and "penchés" adequately translate this effect in the poem. The poet-speaker seeks to make the agitated movement of the tempest visible to the reader by comparing its force to the fury of the sea. He gives it a symbolic dimension in the final line where the trees are bent over the abyss, "Comme sur le puits des enfers" (1: 167, 81.12).

Landscape as a projection of personal emotion and desire is of course an important romantic stylistic device, and a poetic convention often characterized negatively as pathetic fallacy. Here the storm becomes the subjective correlative or correspondence of man's fear of death and eternal suffering. Elements of the landscape–the dungeon, beaten trees, a bloody sky–are clearly projections of the idea of human crime, pain, and the menace of damnation. Gautier's poet has thus transformed Albertus' stormy landscape through the screen of Rosa's picture (probably a depiction of the deluge) into a symbolic, Christian image of man's tragic destiny in a fallen world.

In a one-stanza digression from the narrative of the poem, Gautier's speaker defines the importance of painting as he reflects on the relationship between poetry and its "soeur jumelle":

> Peinture, la rivale et l'égale de Dieu,
> Déception sublime, admirable imposture,
> Qui redonnes la vie et doubles la nature,
> Je ne vous ai pas dit adieu!
>
> (1: 156, 58.9-12)

Its mimetic qualities are seen as deception and imposture in the double oxymoron, for they are splendid but illusionary. Painting is God's rival, nevertheless, since it recreates life and doubles nature; that is, it furnishes life with a new presence and the possibility of significance.

Gautier definitely did not say "adieu" to painting since Raphael emerges as the positive voice in his rich and complex meditation on death and art, *La Comédie de la mort* (1838). Even more certainly than *Albertus*, this poem marks the transition from his flamboyant romantic period to the new directions of the *Emaux et camées*. The tragic figure of death ("prostituée immonde, courtisane éternelle" [2: 49, 16-17]) continues to dominate this work as the poet explores its fatal role in all of life: "La Vie dans la mort" and "La Mort dans la vie" are the major sub-divisions of the poem.

The poet-speaker presents himself as profoundly melancholic, and defines this form of the "mal du siècle" as an interior death. He compares its presence in him to an inner corpse, his mummified aspirations and past loves. After a series of dreams and hallucinations he moves to a more optimistic view, and hopes to replace the obsessive figure of death in his work with a new "muse," the young Grecian beauty immortalized in ancient sculpture. In one of the final stanzas he concludes:

> Loin de moi, cauchemars, spectres des nuits! Les roses,
> Les femmes, les chansons, toutes les belles choses
>   Et tous les beaux amours,
> Voilà ce qu'il me faut. Salut ô muse antique...
>
> (2: 48, 25-28)

This healthy decision to celebrate formal, sensual beauty and reject the obsession with death results from a series of imaginary encounters. The speaker enters into dialogue with major representatives, in the nineteenth-century romantic imagination, of the search for absolutes in life–Faust, Don Juan, Napoleon and Raphael. The first three mythic and historical figures all failed in their search for absolute values that might transcend the limitations of human existence and make of them rivals of the gods. Faust failed in knowledge and science, Don Juan in sensual love, and Napoleon in his quest for power. Only Raphael in his search for ideal beauty succeeded in achieving a kind of immortality for himself and his subjects through painting. The others admit their defeat, and in conventional romantic rhetoric, describe their profound disillusionment with the tragic limits of the human condition.

Raphael succeeds, according to the poet, because he combines love and religious faith. Like the figure of Dürer in Gautier's poem "Melancholia," [7] he represents a time when art served essential, spiritual values and accepted its celebratory role. The figure of Raphael speaks in the poem to criticize the poet's epoch, its loss of energy and especially traditional religious values. In a rather conservative stance Gautier once again seems to blame the melancholy disenchantment of his poet-speaker and his contemporaries on a lack of religious faith, with no attention to current political and social realities.

La Comédie de la mort is yet another meta-poetic text whose conclusion announces the need for the poet to move away from the lugubrious "negative" romanticism of his youth, in terms of theme and style, toward a celebration of formal beauty. The introduction entitled "Portail" presents an already Proustian, prolonged metaphor that compares the evolution in time of the poet's oeuvre to the construction of a cathedral. The outer frame of his work, the "Portail," leads to the decorated tombs, or his early romantic poems, containing the remains of lost illusions:

> Mes vers sont les tombeaux tout brodés de sculpture;
> Ils cachent un cadavre, et sous leurs fioritures
> Ils pleurent bien souvent en paraissant chanter.
> Chacun est le cercueil d'une illusion morte;
> (2: 6, 10-13)

---

[7] See Chapter 2 below, "Reading Melancholy: French Romantic Interpretations of Dürer's Engravings."

Gautier's morbid fascination with death remains in spite of his conscious decision to write a new kind of poetry. His poet-speaker expresses this obsession through the use of a painterly attention to color. He describes the transformations he has accomplished in the representations of the feminine personification of death in his work:

> J'ai changé ton teint vert en pâleur diaphane,
> Sous de beaux cheveux noirs j'ai caché ton vieux crâne,
> Et je t'ai fait la cour.
>
> (2: 46, 16-18)

From deathly green to alabaster white, the figure has been made desirable.

The series of poems entitled *España*, published in the *Poésies nouvelles* (1845), resulted from Gautier's important voyage through Spain from May to October in 1840, and considerably deepens his obsession with death. He discerns its presence in the dessicated landscapes he presents ("In Deserto"), and especially in the Spanish paintings he places in his veritable gallery of transpositions.

As Schick has demonstrated (82-108), Spain becomes in his oeuvre a primary source of poetic practice instead of realistic description; landscapes and paintings become allegories of the inevitability of decay and death. Ribeira, Valdès-Léal and especially Zurbarán exemplify above all for Gautier the Spanish "Weltanschauung," or collective spirit, characterized by an almost morbid religious fervor.

Most of the poems are dialogues between the poet-speaker and the painter, or the subject-other in the painting, transforming them into serious meditations on the presence of death in life. The poem entitled "Ribeira" already suggests "Les Phares" of Baudelaire in its effort to capture the essence of the painter's work, and in its emphasis on the "étrange beauté" (2: 274, 1) to be found in pain and misery.

The originality of the poem, it seems to me, lies in Gautier's effort to produce a psychological analysis of Ribera's style. Critics have mentioned that he perpetuates the cliché about the painter's predilection for scenes of the grotesque, violence, and brutal martyrdom. It is true that he shows no serious interest in the religious paintings of a gentler nature such as Ribera's many depictions of the Madonna and the Christ child.

Gautier in effect seems to have found obsessions corresponding to his own in the Spanish paintings he has chosen. The poem "Ribeira" [Ribera] is constructed as a dialogue, or rather monologue, in which the poet questions the painter and his work in order to discover the profound reasons for the murderous desires revealed in the pictures:

> D'où te vient, Ribeira, cet instinct meurtrier?
> Quelle dent t'a mordu, qui te donne la rage,
> Pour tordre ainsi l'espèce humaine et la broyer?
> (2: 274, 19-21)

Gautier suggests that Ribera's own sadistic pleasure in brutality ("tu sembles enivré par le vin des supplices" [2: 274, 10]) is sublimated into his many scenes of martyrdom; his murderous instincts are transposed into acceptable images of suffering saints.

In his effort to analyze the painter's style in order to understand his psychological motivation, he claims that Ribera tired of his subject matter, "las de l'horrible et des noires couleurs" (2: 275, 13); he tried to use lighter tones and paint soft motifs like Correggio. He was unable, however, to change and continued to serve his obsession, symbolized by the dominance of the color red in his works, "tu ne sus trouver que du rouge de sang" (2: 275, 19).

With "A Zurbarán" Gautier uses dialogue form in an innovative way. The poet-spectator of Zurbarán's paintings enters into a discussion with the subjects of the works chosen; that is, the monks who seem even to enjoy their solitary martyrdom. He attempts to understand their incomprehensible acceptance of suffering and torture, and suggests that they have exaggerated and deformed the Christian sense of the worthlessness of the body's life; he labels their attitude "ce morne suicide" (2: 309, 15).

Essentially a dialogue between poet and painter, since the poem is dedicated to the artist himself, the work does not present a description of a specific painting. Instead it offers a composite of Zurbarán's portraits of monks that Gautier had seen in Seville, and in the Spanish collection at the Louvre even before his travels.[8]

---

[8] Lipschutz, in her article "Théophile Gautier, le musée espagnol et Zurbarán," mentions the importance of the paintings of monks Gautier knew from the "Musée

> Qu'il vous peigne en extase au fond du sanctuaire,
> Du cadavre divin baisant les pieds sanglants,
> Fouettant votre dos bleu comme un fléau bat l'aire,
>
> Vous promenant rêveurs le long des cloîtres blancs,
> Par file assis à table au frugal réfectoire,
> Toujours il fait de vous des portraits ressemblants.
>
> Deux teintes seulement, clair livide, ombre noire;
> Deux poses, l'une droite et l'autre à deux genoux,
> A l'artiste ont suffi pour peindre votre histoire.
>
> Forme, rayon, couleur, rien n'existe pour vous;
> A tout objet réel vous êtes insensibles,
> Car le ciel vous enivre et la croix vous rend fous...
>
> (2: 311, 3-14)

In these stanzas the poet characterizes the painter's work according to its pictorial qualities. The monks obsessed with their spiritual life are realistically portrayed ("portraits ressemblants"), but only two tones are employed. Zurbarán's "dur pinceau les laboure et les creuse" (2: 310, 25) in a violent contrast of black and bright light. Zurbarán's precise, severe line and apparent lack of interest in nuances of color, at least in these paintings, become signs of the monks' total absorption in the spiritual world:

> Le vertige divin, l'enivrement de foi
> Qui les fait rayonner d'une clarté fiévreuse,
> Et leur aspect étrange, à vous donner l'effroi.
>
> (2: 310, 22-24)

The poems in *España* are perhaps the most complex examples of Gautier's "transposition d'art." They are not just efforts to repro-

---

espagnol" (organized during the reign of Louis Philippe) before his trip to Spain. He was especially impressed by the "Saint-François à genoux, une tête de mort entre les mains" (112). In Seville he probably saw the "Repos de Chartreux" which is the source for several lines in his poem "A Zurbarán" (2: 311, 7-9). Lipschutz had already studied the profound influence of Spanish painting on the romantic imagination in a previous work: *Spanish Painting and the French Romantics*. René Jasinski's study in *España* of the major sources of Gautier's poems in this collection should also be consulted.

duce paintings in poetic terms or representations of an imagined landscape, but serious and troubled meditations on death.

Gautier chooses to ignore the real variety of expression and subject matter to be found in the paintings of Ribera and Zurbarán in order to concentrate on the pictorial signs that nourish his personal symbolism. To the Egyptian imagery of mummification (*Roman de la momie*, 1857) and the obsession with "la morte amoureuse" that is found throughout his oeuvre, must be added the living death or death-in-life of the Spanish monk and religious martyrs.

Gautier's concept of the suffering monk was thus formed before his trip to Spain, and this figure became for him an essential element of Spanish religious life. What he discovers in Spain is just the confirmation of an image already fixed by the screen of the paintings. Ilse Lipschutz concludes her article ("T. Gautier, le musée espagnol et Zurbarán") with a quote from Gautier that reveals to what extent the inner "musée imaginaire" dominates his vision, and prevents him from observing nature as it is: "comme cela nous est arrivé plusieurs fois dans notre vie, nous abandonnions la proie pour l'ombre, et le tableau nous empêchait de voir la nature" (117).

To conclude this essay with a closer examination of Gautier's ekphrastic techniques, it is useful to concentrate on the important role of landscape painting in his poetry. He admired Théodore Rousseau and other members of the Barbizon school, and generally preferred their style of romantic nature painting. He is especially favorable to Corot in his critical reviews of the salons (Miquel 1: 85-102). There are many examples throughout his poetic production of efforts to describe actual landscapes ("Paysage," "In Deserto," "Soleils couchants"), and as we have seen, to create imaginary landscapes through the filtering screen of a real painting (Albertus and his model Salvatore Rosa). There are also important efforts to represent or transpose landscapes painted by well known artists such as Watteau and Ernest Hébert.[9] The poems "Paysage" (1830) and

---

[9] In "Watteau" he suggests the atmosphere of the "fêtes galantes" anticipating Verlaine (2: 75). He also "transposed" Ernest Hébert's famous painting "La Malaria" set in a Roman landscape (3: 151).

"A trois paysagistes, salon de 1839" can serve to illustrate this dynamic function of landscape in his work.

The brief four-stanza poem "Paysage," in lines of seven syllables, whose uneven rhythm is undoubtedly intended to support the melancholy tone of the work, evokes the emptiness of a country landscape:

> Pas une feuille qui bouge,
> Pas un seul oiseau chantant,
> Au bord de l'horizon rouge
> Un éclair intermittent;
>
> D'un côté rares broussailles,
> Sillons à demi noyés,
> Pans grisâtres de murailles,
> Saules noueux et ployés;
>
> De l'autre, un champ que termine
> Un large fossé plein d'eau,
> Une vieille qui chemine
> Avec un pesant fardeau;
>
> Et puis la route qui plonge
> Dans le flanc des coteaux bleus,
> Et comme un ruban s'allonge
> En minces plis onduleux.
>
> (1: 6)

The poet-speaker presents a series of impressions without detailed description. It is a devalorized landscape, introduced by the negative "pas" and characterized by absence and negative qualities: the speaker notes a menacing thunderstorm on the horizon, and the willow trees are bent low. He indicates the framing sides of his pictorial representation with "d'un côté" and "de l'autre"; sparse shrubbery half immersed in water on the left, and a field which ends in a watery ditch on the right. The center of the picture is occupied by the path which leads to distant hills. These simple and rather "realistic" notations of a watery landscape are intensified by the use of three colors: the red horizon, grey walls, and the blue hills in the distance. Only one rather banal but appropriate comparison is used to suggest the presence of the viewer who interprets the undulating movement of the road "comme un ruban." There is a solitary personage in this landscape, an old lady walking with a heavy burden who completes the impression of the isolation and sadness of the country.

Precise notations of nature and use of color, clear indications of composition and the spectator's point of view, metaphor as interpretation of the scene: these are the general characteristics of Gautier's reproductions of landscape. The effect on the reader of this depiction of a watery, threatened and devalorized scene is, of course, a feeling of melancholy. This landscape, which René Jasinski (1: xix) links to a remembrance from Gautier's childhood spent at Mauperthuis in the Seine-et-Marne region, is most probably an actual one, and not based on a specific painting. It recalls, however, certain works of T. Rousseau or Millet's scenes of peasant life. It becomes a metaphor for sorrow and loss, an inner landscape, rather than a realistic attempt to describe a natural scene. Just as in "In Deserto" (2: 281-282), a poetic representation of the tragic Spanish countryside, the actual landscape is primarily a source of poetic allegory (Schick 82-108).[10] The dessicated Spanish decor symbolized the aridity of the poet's inner life, his current lack of creative drive. This lonely, watery landscape in "Paysage" is an objective correlative of his melancholic state and evokes the empty reverie of lost childhood. Both landscapes are without an essence, a presence that might give the poem its spiritual value, and a source of potential meaning. What is indeed lacking in these negative, poetic landscapes is the painting-in-the-text, the filter or artistic screen that always seems to provide the poet with a necessary source of idealism and signification, a means to transform observed reality into an ideal image.

The long poem "A trois paysagistes," written in 1839, exhibits an early reaction to the modernization of contemporary French society. The role of the landscape painter, according to Gautier (critic as

---

[10] Michael Riffaterre analyzes "In Deserto" in detail in chap. 1 of his *Semiotics of Poetry*. He explains how semiosis replaces mimesis to produce a symbolic code in which the desert is a sign of artistic sterility.

well as poet), is to represent the beauty of nature, its essence and presence, in an increasingly urban, industrialized society that is already beginning to destroy it. In a clear expression of early environmental concern Gautier addresses his readers: "–Enfants déshérités, hélas! sans la peinture, / Nous pourrions oublier notre mère nature" (2: 225, 17-18).

This important poem for those interested in interarts comparisons appears as a companion piece to Gautier's essays on the official Salons. He describes a series of paintings he had viewed in 1839 by Bertin, Aligny and Corot who had worked together during Corot's first sojourn in Italy (1825-1828). He praises Bertin especially for the precision of his line resembling the pure contours of Ingres. The climax and final section of the poem is reserved for a beautiful and complex transposition of Corot's picture, a passage to be examined in detail:

>   La campagne de Rome, embrasée et féconde,
>   En sillons rutilants jusques à l'horizon
>   Roule l'océan d'or de sa riche moisson.
>   Comme d'un encensoir la vapeur embaumée,
>   Dans le lointain tournoie et monte une fumée,
>   Et le ciel est si clair, si cristallin, si pur,
>   Que l'on voit l'infini derrière son azur.
>   Au-devant près d'un mur réticulaire, en briques,
>   Sont quelques laboureurs dans des poses antiques,
>   Avec leur chien couché, haletant de chaleur,
>   Cherchant contre le sol un reste de fraîcheur;
>   Un groupe simple et beau dans sa grâce tranquille,
>   Que Poussin avoûrait et qu'eût aimé Virgile.
>
>   Mais voici que le soir du haut des monts descend:
>   L'ombre devient plus grise et va s'élargissant;
>   Le ciel vert a des tons de citron et d'orange.
>   Le couchant s'amincit et va plier sa frange;
>   La cigale se tait, et l'on n'entend de bruit
>   Que le soupir de l'eau qui se divise et fuit.
>   Sur le monde assoupi les heures taciturnes
>   Tordent leurs cheveux bruns mouillés des pleurs nocturnes.
>   A peine reste-t-il assez de jour pour voir,
>   Corot, ton nom modeste écrit dans un coin noir.
>
>   (2: 228-229)

Gautier's speaker presents a Corot view of the Roman countryside, most probably "Un soir, paysage," [11] an excellent example of the luminous landscapes he produced after his first stay in Rome. The poet's description, the first step in his usual process of "transposition," soon becomes a narration and finally a symbolic interpretation of the painting.

The formal and structural elements of the landscape depicted are clearly represented as seen from the perspective of the viewer. The horizontal lines of harvest wheat stretch in rows "jusques à l'horizon," there is smoke "dans le lointain," and in the first picture plane, "au-devant," near a brick wall can be observed several laborers arranged in antique poses.

Gautier's speaker reads the painting in time as well as in space. He sees the approach of night in the gray shadows from the hills, and *hears* evening in the sounds evoked by the painting—"la cigale se tait," and "le soupir de l'eau." The forms, colors and sounds correspond to create an impression in the speaker of harmonious nightfall in a pre-Baudelairean example of poetic synesthesia.

He notes and names precise colors and shades, often attributing to them a symbolic value; the harvest is a rich golden sea, and the green sky of the setting sun contains lemon and orange tones. The approaching twilight suggests the mythical hours of the day twisting their dark brown hair.

In fact, the descriptive level of the text is transformed from the very beginning into interpretation through the speaker's use of myth and metaphor. The scene is compared, in a conventional fashion, to a bucolic Virgilian eclogue that Poussin might have treated. The poet thus encodes the work in the valorized and signifying tradition of literary and artistic classicism. This comparison is devel-

---

[11] Corot exhibited two paintings in the Salon of 1839: "Site d'Italie" and "Un soir, paysage." Alfred Robaut, in his *L'Oeuvre de Corot: catalogue raisonné et illustré*, identified the latter work as the pictorial source for this poem of Gautier. The catalogue of the recent retrospective (1996) of Corot's paintings reproduces "Un soir, paysage" (no. 75), and the claim is made that the other landscape of 1839 is no longer identifiable. Michael Pantazzi discusses these paintings in the section entitled "The Greatest Landscape Painter of Our Time." Textual evidence in the poem, however, suggests to me that Gautier conflated and transposed both paintings in his poetic recreation of Corot's work. Figures in "poses antiques," for example, are found in "Site d'Italie" (copied by Robaut) but not in "Un soir, paysage." The latter painting is now entitled "Le batelier, effet du soir," and is in the J. Paul Getty Museum in California.

oped by reference to a series of classical images: the countryside is tan and fecund like "Cérès la blonde," and the smoke in the distance is likened to the perfumed vapors of an incense burner. The laborers in antique poses and the presence of the taciturn figures of the hours participate in the code of spiritual paganism.

These images suggested by the picture lead the speaker to intuit and interpret the essence of the Roman landscape–the promise of fulfillment or perpetually renewed life in the golden ocean of this rich harvest. The central metaphor "océan d'or" combines the poet's view of the bountiful harvest depicted in the painting, and his interpretive vision of its infinite renewal like the ocean, an accepted romantic image of infinity: "Et le ciel est si clair, si cristallin, si pur, / Que l'on voit l'infini derrière son azur" (2: 228, 22-23).

The transposition of Corot's painting into poetry thus furnishes the poet with an allegory of rebirth. The golden harvest becomes a sign of spiritual renewal, under the watchful presence of infinite being, behind and beyond the surfaces of daily life. Corot's painting therefore points to a consoling spiritual truth as it suggests to the poet the mystical image of the "océan d'or." It functions for Gautier's poet-speaker as a screen between the tragic imperfections of modern city life and the desired ideal of the spiritual world. After concluding his representation of this radiant, richly symbolic Roman landscape, he complains: "Nous voici replongés dans la brume et la pluie, / Sur un pavé de boue et sous un ciel de suie" (2: 229, 11-12). And with his customary ability to perceive reality as a painter he notes the reflections in the city streets: "Les ruisseaux miroitants lancent des reflets ternes" (2: 229, 16).

The luminous light and colors have disappeared in the dull environment of the city; the paintings were, above all, an "invitation au voyage." One can easily appreciate Baudelaire's dedication of the *Fleurs du mal* to the master Gautier. The painting and the poem are a source of evasion, and also of possible signification outside of contemporary reality:

> Merci donc, o vous tous, artistes souverains!
> Amants des chênes verts et des rouges terrains,
> Que Rome voit errer dans sa morne campagne,
> Dessinant un arbuste, un profil de montagne,
> Et qui nous rapportez la vie et le soleil

> Dans vos toiles qu'échauffe un beau reflet vermeil!
> Sans sortir avec vous nous faisons des voyages;
> Nous errons, à Paris, dans mille paysages;
> Nous nageons dans les flots de l'immuable azur,
> Et vos tableaux, faisant une trouée au mur,
> Sont pour nous comme autant de fenêtres ouvertes,
> Par où nous regardons les grandes plaines vertes,
> Les moissons d'or, le bois que l'automne a jauni,
> Les horizons sans bornes et le ciel infini!
>
> (2: 226, 3-16)

The painted landscape becomes the source of a spiritual journey of discovery, and painting provides an essential link between the poet and the superior reality he strives to evoke in many poems. A "transposition d'art" is therefore at the same time a description, a poetic re-creation, and a symbolic interpretation of the painting observed or imagined. The painting's function is to be a point of departure or impetus for the poetic impulse, and ultimately a source of signification in the text. The painting-in-the-poem provides a presence or spiritual essence that gives the work its center, its ideal value.

"Le Sommet de la tour" (1838) provides an excellent resume of Gautier's appreciation of his own work before he fully developed the pre-Parnassian aesthetics of the *Emaux et camées*. The poem offers an allegory of the poet's search for artistic perfection and personal recognition as a serious poet. He compares his efforts in poetry to an architect's painstaking creation of a church steeple. Gautier, the romantic idealist, is not yet prepared to define his creative process solely in terms of formal construction and the surface beauty of things and words. He clearly announces his desire to evoke in his poetry a spiritual reality, through and beyond the landscapes he so admires, and which he delights in representing with a painterly eye:

> Du haut de cette tour à grand'peine achevée,
> Pourrai-je t'entrevoir, perspective rêvée,
> Terre de Chanaan où tendait mon effort?
>
> (2: 215)

Chapter 2

READING MELANCHOLY: FRENCH ROMANTIC
INTERPRETATIONS OF DÜRER'S ENGRAVINGS

REPRODUCTIONS of Albrecht Dürer's engravings and drawings were popular and influential during the romantic period in France. His presentations of mysterious forests, grotesque figures and late medieval imagery corresponded to the romantic aesthetic that favored the pre-classical in art. His engravings entitled "The Knight, Death and the Devil" (1513) and especially "Melencolia I" can almost be considered icons of the French romantic imagination. Many writers found their personal feelings of anguish and disenchantment with contemporary society forcefully represented. They were able to project the artist's sense of his destiny to create meaning in chaotic times, his frustration and sense of tragic loss into these complex images.

Dürer himself was appreciated as a figure of troubled genius, a complete artist of the Northern Renaissance whose strong interest in science as well as art and aesthetics prefigured Goethe. His work was seen to bridge the end of the medieval era and the beginning of a new world, a period that seemed to parallel the difficult transition in society from the *Ancien Régime* to the new bourgeois cultures after 1830.

In his study *Dürer in French Letters*, James S. Patty examined the penetration of Dürer the artist and his work in French literature from the sixteenth century to the end of the nineteenth with special emphasis on their importance to romantic poets and prose writers (167-262). Through a valuable, detailed historical survey he analyzes specific texts in the romantic period, from Jules Janin and Balzac to Gautier and Baudelaire, that illustrate Dürer's influence in the formation of the romantic aesthetic.

My interest is primarily in the specific attempt by romantic writers to transpose pictorial techniques and effects into prose and poetry. I plan therefore to limit my discussion to a few major examples of this particular and important case of intertextuality–painting (or rather, engravings) into text.

There are at least four poems of Hugo that are directly related to Dürer's engravings: "Un Dessin d'Albert Dürer" (1827), "A Albert Dürer" (1837), "A quoi songeaient les deux cavaliers dans la forêt" (1853), and "Melancholia" (1846-55). Gautier's poem from 1834, also entitled "Melancholia," compares Dürer's portrait to contemporary expressions of melancholy. Michelet, in section 5 of the *Histoire de France* (Réforme), devotes a chapter to "Albert Dürer, La Melancholia," in which he uses the engraving to symbolize the grandeur and limitations of Renaissance genius. Nerval alluded to the "soleil noir" of Dürer's engraving in his sonnet "El Desdichado" (1853), and in *Aurélia* he describes a dream in which a disheartened androgyne-angel, resembling Dürer's figure, visits a labyrinthine library.

These four readings illustrate different aesthetic perspectives and social preoccupations while illuminating the general romantic attraction to Dürer's masterworks. Some texts can be considered "transpositions d'art" in the nineteenth-century romantic sense of an effort to recreate through one medium the materials from another; others are descriptive, interpretative, or symbolic versions of the original drawing.

The earliest example of Hugo's interest in Dürer is found in his "Un Dessin d'Albert Dürer–Minuit," published posthumously in *Toute la Lyre* but written in 1827 in the style of a German ballad. C. W. Thompson in his study *Victor Hugo and the Graphic Arts (1820-33)* concludes that Hugo may have had a specific drawing (or engraving) in mind when he wrote this work, but it cannot be identified (65-68). Indeed Hugo presents a generalized version of a "danse macabre" with very little pictorial detail; he is primarily concerned with experiments in rhyme and rhythm characteristic of his early *Ballades* (1826).

C. W. Thompson and Jean-Bertrand Barrère conclude that Hugo's interest in Dürer at this early stage was limited to the representation of grotesque figures, the presence of dramatic antithesis in the engravings and a preference for the interaction of light and dark rather than the use of color. Hugo's language in "Un Dessin" recreates an atmosphere of moonlight and shadow that evokes the presence of death; and then the poet's voice interprets the scene in a traditional way:

> Ainsi la mort nous chasse et nous foule,
> Foule
> De héros petits et d'étroits
> Rois.
>
> (*Poésies* 3: 513, 77-80)

"A Albert Dürer" (1837), written ten years later and published in *Les Voix intérieures*, is a much more profound interpretation of Dürer's vision. It can be considered a true "transposition d'art" since it is most probably based on the famous engraving "The Knight, Death, and the Devil." Robert J. Clements comments briefly on Hugo's poem in an interesting comparatist study of five literary readings of Dürer's work, including texts of Borges and Sienkiewicz (1-8). Hugo does not attempt to reproduce linguistically exact elements of the drawing; his aim is rather to interpret its visionary quality. The poet addresses his "maître Albert Dürer, O vieux peintre pensif" (*Oeuvres* 1: 963, 6) directly:

> Une forêt pour toi, c'est un monde hideux.
> Le songe et le réel s'y mêlent tous les deux.
> Là se penchent rêveurs les vieux pins, les grands ormes
> Dont les rameaux font cent coudes difformes,
> Et dans ce groupe sombre agité par le vent
> Rien n'est tout à fait mort ni tout à fait vivant.
> Le cresson boit; l'eau court; les frênes sur les pentes,
> Sous la broussaille horrible et les ronces grimpantes,
> Contractent lentement leurs pieds noueux et noirs.
> Les fleurs au cou de cygne ont les lacs pour miroirs;
> Et sur vous qui passez et l'avez réveillée,
> Mainte chimère étrange à la gorge écaillée,
> D'un arbre entre ses doigts serrant les larges noeuds,
> Du fond d'un antre obscur fixe un oeil lumineux.
> O végétation! esprit! matière! force!
> Couverte de peau rude ou de vivante écorce!
>
> (*Oeuvres* 1: 964, 4-19)

He suggests that they share the same animistic philosophy of nature, alive with the mysterious forces of good and evil. The forest for both Dürer and Hugo is monstrously swarming with signs of obscure meaning. Dürer evokes this mystery through his figures and symbols (the stoic Knight and his horse, Death and the horned Devil) and a compact atmosphere of confusion and menace.

The poet, on the other hand, names the strange effects of nature and personifies its mysterious forces: the pines are "rêveurs," next to the great elms with their twisted branches resembling misshapen elbows. He suggests the perpetual movement of mysterious life through all of nature: "le cresson boit; l'eau court" and the briar are "grimpantes."

His transposition goes far beyond a description of elements in the engraving to become a representation of the awe-inspiring, frightening spirit of material nature that the ordinary person fails to observe. It is indeed the poet's function, according to Hugo, to give voice to the mute aspirations of this complex world. He goes far beyond Dürer's precise and basically realistic presentation to include images of the imaginary such as the strange chimeras clinging to the knotted wood, and staring with an "oeil lumineux" from the depths of a cave. His personifying adjectives suggest fear and unknown life: the oaks are "monstrueux"; terms like "horrible," "confuses," "sauvages," "difformes" characterize elements of the forest.

According to Erwin Panofsky in his celebrated study of Dürer, *The Life and Art of Albrecht Dürer*, this engraving represents the stoic knight passing through the valley of the shadow of death. He typifies the great peril and travails facing the Christian living in the daily world of action and decision. High above him is pictured the seemingly unattainable fortress of the Lord. Hugo pays scant attention to the actual iconography of the engraving; instead he stresses his affinity with the visionary eye of Dürer and his own ability to sense and give voice to the mysteries of nature:

> J'ai senti, moi qu'échauffe une secrète flamme,
> Comme moi palpiter et vivre avec une âme,
> Et rire, et se parler dans l'ombre à demi-voix,
> Les chênes monstrueux qui remplissent les bois.
>
> (*Oeuvres* 1: 64, 26-29)

The poem is thus an early affirmation of Hugo's own visionary project under the aegis of the German master. Many poems of *Les Contemplations* (1856) will develop the same animistic philosophy and attempt to evoke the invisible life of nature without reference to Dürer. This development in Hugo's personal vision of course culminates in the central philosophical poem from the section *Au Bord de l'infini*, "Ce que dit la bouche d'ombre" (1854). The poem is a complex, ambitious attempt to combine pantheistic, Christian and occult elements into a vast cosmic myth of the regeneration of the universe. Hugo traces its transformation from alienation in evil and matter into a world reborn, re-integrated into divine harmony. Critics such as James Patty have suggested that Hugo's central image of the dark cosmic source of meaning, the "bouche d'ombre," may have been related to the black sun attributed to Dürer's engraving "Melencolia I" (184).

Book 4 of *Les Contemplations* (*Pauca meae*) contains one of Hugo's most beautiful ballad-like poems, which to me bears a direct link to the same engraving, "The Knight, Death and the Devil." The poem "A quoi songeaient les deux cavaliers dans la forêt" (1853) might be considered a modern variation on the theme of the hero's perilous journey to spiritual salvation. It also offers another interesting example of romantic "dédoublement" in which the speaker is accompanied on his journey by his companion Hermann, who is, in effect, his alter ego.

The doubling of the personality seems to represent an expression of anguish when the poet is confronted with the possibility of death as "néant." Hermann's spirit is "vide d'espérance" (*Oeuvres*, 2: 655, 8), while the speaker retains his faith in a meaningful afterlife despite the undeniable universality of human suffering, "Et je lui dis: Tais-toi! respect au noir mystère" (2: 656, 11). This meditation on death certainly expresses moments of serious doubt on Hugo's part. Similar themes are found throughout the *Contemplations* dominated by images of unjust suffering and the death of innocence, such as the tragic loss of his daughter Léopoldine.[1]

In his analysis of the engraving Erwin Panofsky affirms that Dürer's steadfast knight seated upon his monumental horse, and

---

[1] In her study of *Les Contemplations* Susanne Nash emphasizes the function of the death of Léopoldine as an organizing principle in the overall structure of the work.

viewed in heroic profile, is totally unaware of the presence of death and the devil in his path. In fact, these weak and pathetic images are only "spooks and phantoms" (152) that cannot impede the knight's spiritual progress. Hugo's two "chevaliers" on the other hand articulate their personal anguish, "Le malheur, c'est la vie" (2: 656, 5); Hermann says, "Je songe à ceux que l'existence afflige" (2: 655, 16) while the speaker repeats like a musical refrain "Je suis plein de regrets" (2: 655, 2-4).

The poem's very musical rhythm and rich use of assonance convey the regular movement of the mysterious ride through the forest, certainly by this time a romantic convention in the tradition of the German ballad. The work's originality lies rather in its pictorial details. Just as Dürer's grotesque and tormented nature suggested the presence of death, Hugo's somber forest reflects the anguish of the two knights and their metaphysical doubts. In nature, however, are contained the double signs of nothingness and rebirth that correspond to the antithesis embodied in the dialogue between Hermann (the skeptic) and the speaker (the reluctant believer). The clouds, for example, are negatively compared to marble tombs, anticipating imagery found in Baudelaire's series of "Spleen" poems;[2] the stars, however, shining through the branches suggest a swarm of "oiseaux de feu" (2: 655, 61), the phoenix of rebirth.

In the only use of color in the poem the woods are named "solitudes vertes" (2: 656, 10); and yet the bushes communicate like old friends, fountains sing, and the oaks murmur. The fountain readily symbolizes life and the oak wisdom; the wind carries the sound of the angelus and therefore is transformed into a spiritual voice. These metaphoric details and personifications not only animate the natural setting in Hugo's usual manner, they capture the ambivalence of the human drama in a simple opposition between death and renascence. According to Hermann, night caresses the dead and the "ciel rayonnant calme toutes les âmes / dans tous les tombeaux à la fois" (2: 656, 19). The poem ends without resolution of the antithesis between fear of nothingness and the hope of salvation; the speaker simply silences his unquiet self, "Tais-toi! respect au noir mystère!" (2: 656, 11).

---

[2] In poem 78 of the *Fleurs du mal* the sky "bas et lourd pèse comme un couvercle/ Sur l'esprit gémissant en proie aux longs ennuis" (96).

Hugo has succeeded beautifully in integrating metaphysical speculation and the representation of a natural scene by endowing elements of nature with an ambivalent, mysterious life. He therefore foregoes the use of allegorical figures or the suggestion of a specific spiritual narrative such as those found in Dürer's engravings. His representation of uncertainty and doubt echoes contemporary controversy about religious values and the loss of belief in traditional dogma early in the nineteenth century. It recalls efforts to rationalize Christian belief in humanitarian or philosophical terms such as can be found in the works of Fourier or Lamennais.

The "Melencolia I" (1514) of Dürer has inspired many artists and writers over the centuries. Paintings and drawings from Domenico Feti to Arnold Boecklin have reproduced and re-interpreted the image of a melancholy woman, and writers including Thomas Mann (*Doctor Faustus*) and Julia Kristeva (*Soleil noir, dépression et mélancolie*) have used it as an important intertextual reference.[3]

The drawing had particular significance for the French romantics for whom melancholy itself became a privileged expression of artistic frustration; the attitude or pose of disenchantment with life was indeed a sign of intellectual superiority from Chateaubriand to Nerval. In *Mélancolie et opposition: les débuts du modernisme en France*, Ross Chambers makes a convincing case for the melancholic text as an important writer's medium to oppose societal pressures especially after the failure of the Revolution of 1848 and the oppressive political strategies of the Second Empire.

Hugo, Gautier, Michelet, and Nerval make intertextual use of the famous engraving in very different ways, but all of them illus-

---

[3] In his study of the function of paintings in a series of important novels, Jeffrey Meyer includes a chapter on Dürer and *Doctor Faustus* of Thomas Mann. Reinhard Kuhn, in *The Demon of Noontide: Ennui in Western Literature*, studies the evolution of expressions of boredom from antiquity to the present. See pp. 75-76 for a discussion of Dürer's engraving. Julia Kristeva's *Soleil noir, dépression et mélancolie* is primarily a psychoanalytical study of the phenomenon of melancholy with many references to literary texts including Nerval. In a recent study of melancholy in Renaissance literature, *The Gendering of Melancholia: Feminism, Psychoanalysis, and the Symbolics of Loss in Renaissance Literature*, Juliana Schiesari argues convincingly that male melancholy was associated with creative genius since the writings of Ficino, but female melancholic states have traditionally been negatively viewed as sickness and neurosis. Dürer's melancholic genius figure is indeed a woman, although an angel. However most of the later interpreters of the engraving presented the artist figure as a man (Michelet) or an androgyne (Nerval).

trate how profoundly this complex image corresponded to personal aspirations and could be interpreted in terms of contemporary cultural constructs.

Hugo's great humanitarian poem "Melancholia" composed between 1846 and 1855, but dated 1838 and placed in the third book (*Les Luttes et les rêves*) of the *Contemplations* makes no direct reference to the engraving other than in its title. It is therefore neither a transposition nor an interpretation of Dürer's engraving itself, but rather an original presentation of the phenomenon of melancholy; its text offers a decidedly modern explanation for the frustration and despair of the artist.

Constructed as a series of small "tableaux" or precise scenes of contemporary Parisian life, it often suggests Daumier's famous caricatures or his paintings of the lower classes. It offers a gallery of portraits, often realistic in detail, of the suffering in modern city life; each one is structured on the simple antithesis between the rich who are in power and the poor who suffer. Portraits of the alcoholic woman, the child worker, the outcast soldier, and the hungry man who steals a loaf of bread present the victims of social injustice, the effects of nascent industrialization and the failure of attempted social reforms. These human "tableaux" surround or frame the expanding symbolic image of the beaten, dying horse, whose accusatory eye has the power to reflect the infinity of incomprehensible suffering in the universe.

The major link with Dürer's engraving is the representation of the disenchanted artist, whose portrait is simply placed among those of the other victims, and who understands that his ideals for society cannot be realized. He is depicted as a poet, a man of genius, and compared in typical romantic fashion to the solitary navigator of a ship: "Le progrès est son but, le bien est sa boussole; / Pilote, sur l'avant du navire il s'isole" (*Oeuvres* 2: 571, 24-25). Through imagery of light Hugo evokes his familiar concept of the creative person as prophet and spiritual guide of society:

> Il contemple, serein, l'idéal et le beau;
> Il rêve; et par moments il secoue un flambeau,
> Qui, sous ses pieds, dans l'ombre, éblouissant la haine,
> Eclaire tout à coup le fond de l'âme humaine...
>
> (2: 571, 10-13)

The artist is in reality, however, misunderstood, mocked, and like Christ dies an ignominious death. The effect of this portrait, intermingled with the other scenes of suffering, is to suggest that the artist's profound melancholy results from the ruin of his dream of social progress. He recognizes that his means of expression are inadequate to influence change in the corrupt social context of failed revolution and the harsh effects of the new capitalist society. The modern city is seen, at the conclusion of the poem, as a breeder of crime, its symbol the guillotine. The last stanzas mark the change from realistic scenes of Parisian life to the poet's dark vision of social injustice based on the metaphor "peuple/océan":

> L'indigence, flux noir, l'ignorance, reflux,
> Montent, marée affreuse, et, parmi les décombres,
> Roulent l'obscur filet des pénalités sombres.
> (2: 575, 30-32)

> Le crime, antre béant, s'ouvre dans ces ténèbres;
> Le vent secoue et pousse, en ses froids tourbillons,
> Les âmes en lambeaux dans les corps en haillons;
> Pas de coeur où ne croisse une horrible chimère.
> (2: 575, 36-39)

Théophile Gautier's poem also entitled "Melancholia" (1834) could be compared with his other "transpositions d'art" such as his "portrait gallery" of the Spanish masters Zurbarán and Ribera.[4] His efforts at pictorial representation based on actual paintings were probably the most influential on later writers, including, of course, the many examples of this poetic device to be found in Baudelaire's poetry and poems in prose.[5]

Baudelaire, however, always insisted that the poem must be a re-creation and never a mere description of the work at its source.

---

[4] Théophile Gautier's poems based on paintings are found in his *Poésies diverses* and *Poésies nouvelles*, especially in the section entitled España in vol. 2, *Poésies complètes*.

[5] Many of Baudelaire's poems and prose poems have identifiable links to paintings. Examples are "Les Phares," "Les Bohémiens en voyage" (Callot), "Sur Le Tasse en prison" (Delacroix), "Lola de Valence" (Manet). Many other works allude to paintings or borrow pictorial effects: "Les Plaintes d'un Icare" (Bruegel), "Duellum" (Goya).

His "master" Gautier most often includes an effort to describe the painting, and in "Melancholia" he transforms this description of the engraving into a portrait of Dürer himself. After a lengthy introduction to the differences between the sensual, even "pagan" art of the Italian Renaissance and the spiritual purity of German, "pre-raphaelite" art, Gautier's speaker addresses Dürer directly: "O mon peintre Chrétien!" (*Poésies* 2: 86, 8). He imagines a portrait of the painter based on the engraving, "Il me semble te voir au coin de ta fenêtre" (2: 86, 26), and presents the engraving itself as an autoportrait, a representation of Dürer.

> Tu t'es peint, O Dürer! dans ta Mélancolie,
> Et ton génie en pleurs, te prenant en pitié,
> Dans sa création t'a personnifié.
>
> (2: 87, 4-6)

This would at first appear to be a typical romantic convention, or fallacy, the constant desire to find in the work a reflection of its author. Curiously enough, the great art historian Erwin Panofsky would in essence agree with Gautier. He claims, however, that the engraving "reflects the whole of Dürer's personality rather than a single experience" (171). Dürer himself was a melancholic in every sense of the word. He knew the "inspirations from above," and knew the feeling of "powerlessness and dejection" (171). He was above all an artist-geometrician, who suffered acutely from an awareness of the very limitations of the arts and science he cultivated and loved.

Gautier's description of the engraving is objectively precise in detail but his speaker frequently interprets the angel's melancholy through metaphor and commentary, both direct and indirect:

> Pas un muscle ne bouge: on dirait que la vie
> Dont on vit en ce monde à ce corps est ravie.
> Et pourtant l'on voit bien que ce n'est pas un mort.
> Comme un serpent blessé son noir sourcil se tord,
> Son regard dans son oeil brille comme une lampe,
> Et convulsivement sa main presse sa tempe.
>
> (2: 87, 15-20)

The disorderly arrangement of the objects used in geometry and the arts, especially architecture, is compared to Faust's study, and the famous image of the black sun makes its appearance:[6]

> Le vieux père océan lève sa face morne,
> Et dans le bleu cristal de son profond miroir
> Réfléchit les rayons d'un grand soleil tout noir.
> (2: 88, 1-3)

According to the art historians, however, what we see in the engraving is not a sun at all, but a comet. A person of melancholic temperament was considered to be endowed with prophetic power, and could foresee natural disasters such as the unexpected arrival of a comet on earth. The presence of the comet in the engraving thus reinforces the suggestion of impending doom. The celebrated image of the black sun is therefore based on mis-readings of the picture.

Gautier concludes his representation of the engraving, by developing an antithesis between Dürer's "authentic" version of the artist's melancholy and the pettiness of contemporary imitations, or simulacra, to use Baudrillard's formulation:[7]

> Voilà comme Dürer, le grand maître Allemand,
> Philosophiquement et symboliquement,
> Nous a représenté, dans ce dessin étrange,
> Le rêve de son coeur sous une forme d'ange.
> Notre Mélancolie, à nous, n'est pas ainsi.
> (2: 88, 10-14)

Without referring to precise painters or specific works, Gautier parodies current representations of melancholy "à la mode." His figure of modern "mélancolie" is neither an angel nor a male artist but a stylish "petite-maîtresse" (2: 88, 28); he satirizes the falsity of her attitudes, insincere sentiments, and the need to transform all

---

[6] James S. Patty makes a convincing case for Gautier as the poet who initiated the use of this important image (197-202).

[7] Gautier presents current forms of melancholic expression as inferior simulations of past models; he would appear to anticipate aspects of Baudrillard's explanation of a post-modernist aesthetic attitude toward reality.

emotion into anecdote and fiction: "Chaque pleur de ses yeux se cristallise en conte; / Avec chaque soupir elle souffle un roman" (2: 89, 10-11).

Through this deprecating, gendered portrait of a melancholy woman he accuses his contemporaries of lacking depth of feeling. He attributes this weakness to an excess of rationalism and a subsequent loss of religious faith in his society. The poem's overt message is contained in the phrase, "La passion est morte avec la foi" (2: 89, 25). Dürer's engraving is thus seen as the paradigm of a passionate engagement with the limitations of life and art, and the constant presence of death. Gautier's parodic portrait [8] of contemporary mores suggests the superficiality and emptiness of the lives of women and men without idealism, energy or desire:

> Rien ne vit plus en nous, nos amours et nos haines
> Sont de pâles vieillards sans force et sans vigueur,
> Chez qui la tête semble avoir pompé le coeur.
> (2: 89, 22-24)

His speaker concludes the poem with a generalized expression of melancholy that evokes Freud's definition in "Mourning and Melancholy." The loss that is at the source of grief and authentic disenchantment with life is, for Gautier, that of the richness of the past. Gautier's world in 1834 is an exhausted one, increasingly skeptical about traditional values and the consolation of religious faith. The image of the black sun linked to the engraving has become the worn-out star:

> Mais le soleil vieillit, son baiser moins vermeil
> Glisse sans les chauffer sur nos fronts, et ses flammes
> Comme sur les glaciers, s'éteignent sur nos âmes.
> (2: 89, 27-29)

Although the speaker does not mention the collapse of political ideals, his text recalls Musset's *Confession d'un enfant du siècle* (1834) in which the hero's "mal du siècle" is in large measure attrib-

---

[8] Many of Gautier's texts parody romantic models and satirize contemporary mores. See my *Paradigm and Parody: Images of Creativity in French Romanticism*, ch. 7, on Gautier and the romantic aesthetic.

uted to the failure of the "fathers." The collapse of political systems in the Revolutionary period, Empire and Restauration, has left the young generation with the tragic sense of the impossibility of any real change or progress. A veritable abyss, according to Musset, separates the past from the future. Gautier, for his part, compares his epoch to a mountain volcano now covered with snow. This image effectively evokes the recent energy of the Revolution of 1830 unfortunately spent without significant progress toward democracy or social justice for the lower classes. He returns to Christian imagery in the last lines with a final reference to the angel of Dürer's engraving:

> Mais, hélas! il n'est pas pour nous d'aube nouvelle,
> Et la nuit qui nous vient est la nuit éternelle.
> De nos cieux dépeuplés il ne descendra pas
> Un ange aux ailes d'or pour nous prendre en ses bras.
> (2: 90, 6-9)

Through his insistence on the loss of religious values as the deep source of his generation's supposedly "authentic" melancholy, Gautier avoids direct criticism of the new bourgeois regime of Louis-Philippe. His melancholic text is therefore oppositional and critical of contemporary society, to use Ross Chambers' terminology, but not confrontational. Pale reminders of past spiritual aspiration, this "reflet du passé" (2: 89, 34), or nostalgia for lost faith are certainly acceptable forms of regret in 1834. Direct protest against the failure of his society to realize revolutionary goals for social reform would probably have provoked government censorship.

In section 5 of the *Histoire de France* devoted to the Protestant Reformation, Michelet uses Dürer's engraving "Melencolia I" to symbolize the spirit of the Renaissance. A frequent technique used in his historical writings is the selection of a work of art or architectural monument to summarize an historical event or period. His analysis of the development of the cathedral in the *Histoire de France*, for example, is intended to exemplify the rise and wane of medieval culture in general. Dürer himself is presented by Michelet as the profound conscience of the German people in a period of revolt and violence; his engraving is seen as the very emblem of "le génie de la Renaissance, l'ange de la science et de l'art, couronné de laurier" (415).

In his usual breathless style, marked by exclamations and interrogatives, Michelet interprets the engraving through the invention of a fiction. Much like Diderot in his *Salons* Michelet lets the picture create a story, and even gives a voice to the melancholy figure.

According to Michelet, Dürer's personal disappointment with his own artistic efforts to express the profound spirituality of Christ's life produced this expression of disillusionment: "Il variait ce thème à l'infini, sans satisfaire son coeur, impuissant et vaincu par les réalités dans cette lutte laborieuse: Melancholia" (415).

Michelet, in romantic fashion, sees the creation of the famous engraving as a truly original work, "faisant appel au moi sans appui du passé" (415). He ignores, however, the tradition of the depiction of the melancholic temperament and the figure of geometria that Dürer has successfully combined. Panofsky describes the engraving in the following manner:

> Thus Dürer's most perplexing engraving is, at the same time, the objective statement of a general philosophy and the subjective confession of an individual man. It fuses, and transforms, two great representational and literary traditions, that of Melancholy as one of the four humors and that of Geometry as one of the Seven Liberal Arts. It typifies the artist of the Renaissance, who respects practical skill, but longs all the more fervently for mathematical theory–who feels "inspired" by celestial influences and eternal ideas, but suffers all the more deeply from his human frailty and intellectual finiteness. It epitomizes the Neo-Platonic theory of Saturnian genius as revised by Agrippa of Nettesheim. But in doing all this it is in a sense a spiritual self-portrait of Albrecht Dürer. (171)

One might claim, nevertheless, that Dürer has succeeded in giving a new form to the essential Renaissance paradox of the grandeur and limitations of man's aspirations. Michelet's genius or giant in the engraving is surrounded with the tools of art and architecture, aware of the great possibilities of human creativity. He appears to dream of the unattainable–ideal beauty or absolute truth, the very secret of life. A kind of Faustian man or Balzacian searcher for the absolute, he is, however, eminently aware of his potential for destruction. Michelet's narrator addresses the imaginary figure (to whom he refers as a man) "Oh! fils de la lumière, que tu es triste!...et attristant!...Moi, j'avais cru que la lumière, c'était la joie!" (416). In this unexpected dialogue the figure from the engraving explains the destructive nature of his attempts to transform matter and nature into ideal forms; referring to the irregular block of marble next to him he says: "Prismatique il était, régulier, harmonique. Qu'ai-je fait! Sans arriver à l'art, j'ai brisé la nature" (416). The dog lying near him, he claims, has died as a result of his unsuccessful experiments.

The narrator concludes that the image is one of complete discouragement "qui supprime l'espoir, ne promet rien, pas même sur l'enfance. Le présent est mauvais, mais l'avenir est pire" (417-418). Michelet develops the romantic concept of a world of inner infinity; the genius figure realizes that the infinite he has been seeking through external matter can only be found within himself. He becomes finally a "captif, lié de sa pensée" (417), "la lumière qu'il adore, c'est celle qui est au fond de l'être" (417).

Michelet extends this expression of melancholic disenchantment to include his own generation of thinkers: "nous avons trop entassé! nous succombons sous nos puissances. Celui-ci est captif de l'encombrement de la science" (417). He is undoubtedly alluding to his exhaustive efforts to express the very soul of France through the immense quantity of material documentation studied, and detailed research undertaken during the thirty-year preparation of his texts.

Dürer's angel, like the romantic artist in Michelet's view, understands the difficult, perhaps impossible task of transforming matter into ideal form; the techniques and means of his arts are inadequate to his goals. Matter resists idealization, just as Hugo's modern city in "Melancholia" contradicts his dream of social progress. In his description of the engraving Michelet includes the small child-angel diligently working his stone. He interprets this figure as a symbol of the humble German artisan contrasted with the master, the "ange terrible" (417) lost in his theoretical conceptions. He develops the parallel to suggest that the two angels represent complementary aspects of Dürer's own personality: the conscientious, strong-willed worker and the conceptual thinker.[9] Theory and practice, which are the two necessary components of all creativity, are, however,

---

[9] Erwin Panofsky develops the same symbolism in his interpretation of the two figures (164).

seen here in failure: "Hélas! L'effort n'est pas la force. Si ce géant ne peut, que peut le nain?" (417).

In the final paragraph, concluding his interpretation of Dürer's thought, Michelet contributes to the myth of the "soleil noir." In an ironic gesture of bitterness and revolt against his condition, the artist, according to Michelet, placed a bat against the sun "qui vole outrageusement en pleine lumière, inscrivant la nuit dans le jour, et le mot: Melancholia" (418).

In Gérard de Nerval's works there are several significant allusions to Dürer's engraving "Melencolia I." Ross Chambers' study in *Mélancolie et opposition* of the social framework of madness and melancholy in *Aurélia* affirms that the novella was in effect written under the sign of Dürer's engraving. Julia Kristeva thoroughly analyzes Nerval's sonnet "El Desdichado" in her psychoanalytical study of melancholy, *Soleil noir, dépression et mélancolie*, itself an homage to both Nerval and the persistence of Dürer's iconography. The famous sonnet presenting the speaker-poet's sense of inconsolable loss includes the celebrated lines that resonate throughout Nerval's works: "Ma seule *étoile* est morte, – et mon luth constellé / Porte *le soleil noir de la Mélancolie*" (1: 694, 3-4).

One could justly say that Nerval was haunted by the image of the black sun and the androgynous figure of the angel. In several of his autobiographical works he describes his observation of a black sun in an empty sky.[10] In Nerval's final masterpiece *Aurélia* the first dream presented by the narrator in part I, chapter 2 describes the arrival of the androgyne outside of the labyrinthine rooms and corridors of a vast school: "Vêtu d'une robe longue à plis antiques, il ressemblait à l'Ange de la *Mélancolie* d'Albrecht Dürer" (1: 758).

This dream, in the logic of the text, constituted a confirmation in the narrator's mind that Aurélia's death or his own had been announced to him ("Ma seule *étoile* est morte"). The androgynous figure, "Un être d'une grandeur démesurée, – homme ou femme, je ne sais" (1: 758), appears lost and without energy. He/she falls in

---

[10] For example, Nerval in his *Voyage en Orient*, chapter 2, 1, "Les Femmes du Caire," describes his complex impressions of sunrise in the orient: "Le soleil noir de la mélancolie, qui verse des rayons obscurs sur le front de l'ange rêveur d'Albert Dürer se lève aussi parfois aux plaines lumineuses, comme sur les bords du Rhin, dans un froid paysage d'Allemagne" (2: 151-152).

the middle of a dark courtyard "accrochant et froissant ses ailes le long des toits et des balustres" (1: 758).

In the thematic structure of the text the dream reveals the tragic impossibility for the narrator to attain the profound spiritual knowledge he seeks: the certainty of immortality and proof of the eternal life of his beloved, Aurélia. The lessons and philosophical discussions in the dream academy seem to be monotonous and memorized, unenlightening. The angel who presumably comes from a mystical realm can make no contact with the human world of reason with its limited access to knowledge. The dream thus resembles the situation in Dürer's drawing; Nerval's androgyne cannot communicate its superior awareness of reality and is sadly defeated in the human domain, just as Dürer's angel cannot transform the materials before him into a representation of his ideal vision.

The mystical quality of Nerval's androgyne is signified by its brilliant colors, much like Biblical figures in Blake's drawings: "il était coloré de teintes vermeilles, et ses ailes brillaient de mille reflets changeants" (1: 758). A realization, however, of the angel's impotence in spite of its beauty causes the narrator to awaken from his dream in cries of anguish and despair.

Laurence M. Porter offers a convincing psychoanalytic reading of this dream of the androgyne in his study "Mourning and Melancholia in Nerval's *Aurélia*." The angelic figure would represent in his view a whole or total self (a kind of Jungian archetype) whose collapse signifies the narrator's blocked psychic development. The resultant loss of identity produces the intense feelings of melancholy that pervade the narrator's quest for spiritual truth throughout the text.

Dürer's engraving had an especial appeal to the romantic writers considered here because it seemed above all to reflect their understanding of their situation as artists. The engraving of the melancholy angel is itself auto-reflective, presenting as it does the creative person confronting the limitations of his art and science. Dürer apparently understood, as did the romantics, that melancholy is inseparable from the creative process. The desire to create a new object of beauty, to realize a vision of life, or to give form to a sense of personal identity–in poetry, history or fiction–is always accompanied by disillusionment with current forms of expression, frustration before the intransigence of the materials to be transformed, and nostalgia for lost time. Melancholy produces a curious and critical doubling of the personality. Happiness or the ideal are situated in the elsewhere of the past or the future; the present is the source of anguish and disenchantment. The creative person strives to fashion an image of his ideal world but an important element of the self is drawn to images of sadness and loss. Melancholy is, after all, the contradictory pleasure of those who have no other, the pleasure-in-sadness that ultimately reveals the presence of death in all of life.

CHAPTER 3

GEORGE SAND'S AESTHETIC DREAM: ARTISTS AND ARTISANS IN *LES MAITRES MOSAISTES*

GEORGE Sand's first sojourn in Italy (1833-1834) resulted in a group of novels and short stories with Italian themes and characters,[1] and greatly enriched her love and knowledge of art. The fictionalized account of her experience with Alfred de Musset in Italy, *Elle et lui* (1858), has been frequently studied. Almost no serious attention, however, has been given to her important novel dealing with artist figures and aesthetic issues, *Les Maîtres mosaïstes* (1837), written after her return to Nohant.

Sand's love of music has been well documented;[2] too much emphasis has perhaps been given to her relationship with Chopin, and not enough consideration to the originality of her literary production. Few readers seem aware that *Les Maîtres sonneurs* (1853), her well-known pastoral novel concerning music, has a companion piece that treats the community of artisan, mosaic makers of Venice in the last years of the sixteenth century.

Elle et lui and *Les Maîtres mosaïstes* are the major novels in Sand's oeuvre that present visual artists or painters as protagonists. Her interesting fictional account of the revolutionary events around 1830 entitled *Horace* (1841) also features a painter, Paul Arsène. He

---

[1] In her thorough study of the importance of Italy on Sand's life and works, Annarosa Poli devotes several pages to the genesis of *Les Maîtres mosaïstes* (171-181). She also discusses the other Venetian novels and short stories that resulted from Sand's trip to Venice (e.g., *Mattea, Leone Leoni*). Poli also published an edition of *Les Maîtres mosaïstes* in 1966.

[2] One of the most interesting studies is Marie-Paule Rambeau's *Chopin dans la vie et l'oeuvre de George Sand.*

belongs to the working class, however, and soon discovers that he must give up his desire to paint in order to survive. In *Elle et lui* the characters representing Sand and Musset have been transposed from writers to portrait painters; there is very little development of aesthetic issues in this account primarily devoted to the disintegration of a great passion. George Sand did write important letters about artists; she also composed serious essays praising Ingres, the engraver Calamatta, and Raphael, that can be found in the collection entitled *Questions d'art et de littérature* (1878). Her memoir *Histoire de ma vie* (1854) contains a very perceptive discussion of her great friend Delacroix, whose work she admired and appreciated (2: 250-264). It is my contention, however, that in the novel *Les Maîtres mosaïstes* she represented her ideas on art and aesthetics in a more original fashion, and effectively recreated her humanitarian vision of artistic community through the image of the Renaissance guild.

As will become clear, the uneasy, problematic relationship between the artisan and the painter of "high art" is a major theme in this text, and the techniques of mosaic making can even be read as a meaningful metaphor for novelistic creation. The mosaics created by the historical figures, the Zuccati brothers, found in St. Mark's basilica, that are based on cartoons of Titian and Tintoretto, are transposed in the novel into textual images of the creative process.

In the foreword (Notice) to the 1852 edition of *Les Maîtres mosaïstes*, Sand explains that she wrote the novel for her son, Maurice. She based it on a "fait réel dans l'histoire de l'art" (1), the famous trial of the mosaic makers, which she claims to have embellished only slightly. There is no love plot, she states, because it might upset her son's delicate sensibilities, and therefore, women play almost no role in Sand's fiction about artists in the late Renaissance. In any case, they would have undoubtedly been excluded from membership in the associations of artisans and workers.

The work is an unusually fine example of the richness and variety of Sand's novelistic techniques. It offers a complex narrative structure in which the various characters, artists and artisans, represent a wide range of viewpoints on art and the creative process. Isabelle Naginski, in her excellent study of Sand's novels, emphasizes the experimental and innovative aspects of these works, and especially the use of dialogic and multi-voiced narratives to present conflicting ideas. As both Naginski and Naomi Schor affirm, the novels should generally be read in a tradition outside the development of the mimetic, realist novel. Ideas are transformed into fictional material, and an idealist philosophy, in this case, an aesthetic, emerges from the rich variety of viewpoints represented and symbolized.

There are, nevertheless, important parallels to be found with Balzac's "philosophical" fictions especially those about artists such as *Le Chef d'oeuvre inconnu* (1831). This short story features historical painters like Poussin and Mabuse as well as the fantastic, imaginary protagonist, Frenhofer, and develops the problematic elements of important aesthetic questions. Balzac's text has been interpreted as a representation of the contemporary artistic debate between partisans of Ingres (emphasis on classical line and the formalist tradition), and those who favored Delacroix (color and the imaginative recreation of reality). This artistic conflict is indeed at the center of Frenhofer's anguished and ultimately tragic search for perfection in painting. His efforts to combine and transcend the two traditions in the creation of a superior art form result in the destruction of his masterwork. Sand greatly admired her friend Balzac; she wrote an illuminating essay about their relationship and his creative process in the *Histoire de ma vie* (2: 133-147). Unlike Balzac, however, she is less interested in the description of concrete details in her historically based novel about artists. Her primary concern is the interplay of characters and ideas that affords the plot its various meanings. The "quelques ornements" that she claims to have added to the realistic base of *Les Maîtres mosaïstes* (1) are essentially poetic description, metaphors and symbols of artistic concepts, and aesthetic discourse.

In the novel's preface, addressed to her son Maurice, Sand explains that the anecdote upon which it is based was related to her by the Abbé Panorio during her stay in Venice. The trial of the master mosaic makers, the Zuccati brothers, who were imprisoned after having been accused of utilizing inferior materials in their work, was in reality a well documented historical event.

The third person narrator from Nohant replaces the Abbé as omniscient narrator. He presents a panoply of artistic voices, including those of Titian and Tintoretto who speak and play major roles in the development of the plot.[3] The characters in the novel constitute a paradigm of responses to the problems of artistic creativity. The Zuccati brothers, Francesco and Valerio, the protagonists in the book, share a strong bond of love and mutual admiration, but are nevertheless vividly contrasted by the narrator. Francesco believes that mosaic making is high art, not just the mechanical reproduction of models prepared by great artists like Titian. He is a melancholy idealist, afflicted with a recognizably romantic "mal du siècle," in this late Renaissance period that the narrator characterizes as an age of decadence. His brother, Valerio, a "realist" who is commercially successful with his designs for fashionable clothing, is a happy sensualist, in love with a beautiful woman, and endowed with a rich imagination and uncommon, creative talent.

Another readily recognizable romantic figure is Bozza, the apprentice artist in the Zuccati guild of mosaic makers; he is presented as a "raté" whose feelings of inadequacy and resentment spoil his talent, preventing him from achieving a masterwork. He can be situated in a long line of such failed artistic figures from Vigny's flute player (in "La Flûte")[4] to Balzac's tragic but mediocre poet, Lucien de Rubempré (*Illusions perdues*), and Zola's genetically flawed painter, Claude Lantier (*L'Oeuvre*). His personal suffering eventually turns to envy and jealousy, and it is he who gives the plot its impetus by betraying the Zuccati brothers to their rivals.

Their rivals, the Bianchini brothers, who lead the other union of mosaicists, are portrayed as opportunistic artisans, inferior in talent and concerned only with personal advancement. From motives of hatred and greed, they convince the ruling authorities to bring to trial the Zuccati brothers who work near them in St. Mark's Basilica.

The betrayal of the Zuccati by Bozza and the Bianchini brothers introduces a theme that adds special resonance to the novel. Sand's narrator expresses nostalgia for a time before the decadent period

---

[3] Alfred de Musset's short story *Le Fils du Titien* (1838) also features the great painter, but concentrates on his son, Titianello, who decides that love and life are preferable to the suffering necessitated by a total commitment to great art.

[4] Alfred de Vigny's poem perhaps expresses best the romantic version of the failed artist, whose talent and material possibilities are unfortunately inadequate to his lofty ideals and great ambition. "Du corps et non de l'âme accusons l'indigence. / Des organes mauvais servent l'intelligence" (1: 202).

of this end of century, when artists were able to collaborate, and painters and mosaic makers worked together to produce beauty for spiritual, religious goals. Although this novel was written before her series of utopian works (e.g., *Le Compagnon du tour de France* [1840]), it promotes a past and perhaps lost ideal of artistic community. It evokes a time when craftsmen were appreciated as artists, and renowned artistic figures played a positive role in society as intellectual and moral guides. The romantic ideal of the humanitarian function of the influential artist is represented by the supportive actions of Titian and Tintoretto in the text.

They defend the Zuccati brothers at their trial and are eventually responsible for their rehabilitation; clearly they symbolize the truly great artist capable of understanding the genius of others and exerting a moral influence on his society. In a speech given before the Venetian authorities, Titian praises the mosaicists as true artists who must know and implement the complex laws of painting: design, composition and color harmony. They do not just copy the works of others, they recreate them imaginatively in another medium. They are, in effect, practicing the technique of ekphrasis or "transposition d'art" as it would be named by Gautier and the romantics. Painting is transposed into mosaic, thereby illuminating and enriching the original work of art. This process is thus an excellent illustration of Baudelaire's later formulation of the essential correspondence between the arts that results from a fundamental unity, or universal analogy, among elements of the sensorial world (color, sound, aroma and form) and that of mind and spirit. The interrelationships developed in the arts of music, painting and literature, in the romantic view, function to enrich each medium, and move toward the ideal of a total art form such as that prescribed by Wagner for opera.

The influence of romantic humanitarianism, and specifically Sand's admiration for contemporary socialist thinkers such as Pierre Leroux, is quite evident in this evocation of the late sixteenth-century restorations of the Basilica of St. Mark. For the narrator, a climate of injustice and materialism seems unfortunately to have replaced the communal spirit and artistic cooperation of the previous century. The authentic values emphasized in the text are primarily fraternal association and spiritual idealism; the corporation or guild of the craftsmen mosaic makers represents Sand's ideal of an artistic fraternity whose goal is to create beauty in a community enriched with religious values. Individual egoism and avarice (personified by Bozza and the Bianchini brothers), as well as governmental tyranny, unfortunately work to destroy the harmonious balance of creative forces and communal life.

Musset compared the philistine, bourgeois monarchy of Louis Philippe to Medici Florence in *Lorenzaccio* (1834), a distinguished romantic drama whose model was indeed a text by Sand, *Une Conspiration en 1537* (1831). In a similar manner she suggests parallels between the authoritarian government of Republican Venice and the bourgeois regime that imposed constraints upon writers and artists after the July Revolution of 1830 in France. A major theme in the novel is the need for artistic freedom of expression, and particularly freedom from governmental control over the arts. The Zuccati brothers are condemned by the "Procurateur" or ruling official in charge of overseeing the restorations of the Basilica, essentially because they dared to innovate. They began to use materials like wood (when only enamel and precious stones were permitted), and created figures and motifs from their own imagination, thus declaring themselves to be artists in their own right, and not just imitators.

The imprisonment of Francesco and Valerio, falsely accused of fraud and deception, gives to the novel its romantic, mythopoeic structure. Sand's narrator posits a mythical level to the text, first through reference to Faust and the devil: Bozza, the failed artist, is tempted to betray the brothers Zuccati by the diabolical figure of Vincent Bianchini. The prison experience, placed at the center of the novel, provides yet another example of the romantic use of the initiatory rite of passage, or rebirth pattern, to give the text a spiritual level of meaning. Victor Brombert, in *La Prison romantique*,[5] studied the romantic paradox of the prison, which becomes a source of personal renewal and even individual freedom in many texts of the period from Hugo's *Le Dernier jour d'un condamné* to Stendhal's *La Chartreuse de Parme*.

In the case of *Les Maîtres mosaïstes* the death-in-life, which characterizes the time spent in prison, is reinforced and symbolized by the deadly presence of the plague in Venice, and the pestilential

---

[5] There is, however, no chapter on Sand's work in Brombert's study.

air of the tomb-like, underground cells. The suffering that the brothers endure, almost leading to the death of Francesco, becomes, nevertheless, a source of spiritual renewal. Both brothers are transformed by the experience, and brought to a superior understanding of their creative powers; eventually, after release from prison, they achieve a life in art at a higher level than in their previous existence. The traditional pattern of the universal rite of passage that forms the rebirth myth (as described by Jung and others) gives a clear narrative structure to the experience: (1) with the death of the superficial life of the past, Francesco resolves his doubts concerning his abilities as an artist, and Valerio renounces his frivolous, material preoccupations as he literally nurses his saintly brother in an act of total repudiation of his narcissistic self; (2) the intense suffering of the brothers produces a re-discovery of their inner creative forces; and finally (3) a sense of rebirth from death and the past leads to their success as artists after liberation from prison and to their ultimate recognition by the community. The romantic cliché of the wounded artist, or the need for suffering to produce great art, central to many of Musset's texts such as the poetic cycle of "Les Nuits," is here given a rich and complex fictional treatment. The archetypal rebirth myth thus underlies the novel's narrative structure and provides the text with its deepest significance.

Lucienne Frappier-Mazur discusses the important psychological phenomenon of "dédoublement" or doubling of the personality found in Sand's *Histoire de ma vie*. Her troubled relationships with her plebeian mother and the aristocratic grandmother who raised her apparently created a division in her character that is projected in many novels in terms of female figures with a double (e.g., *Indiana* and *Lélia*), and into fictional situations of class conflict. With reference to Freud and Julia Kristeva, Lucienne Frappier-Mazur studies the difficult movement toward the integration and unification of Sand's own personality as it is recorded in her autobiography.

It seems to me that the brothers Zuccati can be meaningfully included in the paradigm of doubles found in Sand's novels. Valerio, the energetic, sensual brother, the "mauvais sujet," lived in the world like a plebeian, and then devotes all of his energy to his sick brother, as if he were his mother, when they are both imprisoned.

The real mother is absent from their lives (in the novel), and their father disapproves their choice of profession. He is embarrassed by their desire to make mosaics, which he considers to be an artisanal occupation beneath their station in life. Francesco, the solitary idealist, is the melancholy opposite or double of his brother, who is, however, saved by Valerio's total love and devotion during their period of suffering in prison.

The brothers are finally united and integrated into a kind of complete or whole personality when they both present paintings for the final contest in the novel. They are judged by Titian, who functions here as a Jungian great man or universal sage, to be the best artists in their field. He thus provides the approval their father had always denied them and vindicates their choice of profession. Their development toward the realization of a whole, ideal personality is effectively symbolized by the two archangels they created as mosaics for the central vault of the Basilica, for which they themselves are the models. This creation through which they have redeemed themselves, by affirming their spiritual, "angelic" nature, is judged a masterpiece by the jury. At the end of the novel Valerio has accepted his responsibility as a serious artist, and Francesco returns to the world of work with renewed confidence. The Bianchini brothers, who also represent negative alter-egos or bad doubles of the Zuccati men, are not characterized individually in the text.

An important analogy can be made between the mosaic makers of this novel and Sand's conception of the artist as craftsman. Throughout her life she was impressed with the creative person as worker or maker of art. In her autobiographical writings and travel literature such as the *Lettres d'un voyageur* (1834-36), she expressed special admiration for work done traditionally by women and artisans: embroidery and weaving, majolica pottery that she observed in Italy, and especially the mosaics. In a description of her visit to Florence, for example, Sand gives little attention to the paintings of great artists, and indeed states her preference for artisanal objects.[6]

---

[6] In *La Notion d'artiste chez George Sand*, Madeleine L'Hôpital offers a chapter on Sand's admiration for artisanal work and its values (162-170); included is a brief treatment of *Les Maîtres mosaïstes* (167-170). In a more recent, feminist study, "Arachnologies: The Woman, the Text and the Critic," in *Subject to Change*, Nancy K. Miller develops the relationships between weaving and writing, especially for women writers in the 19th century. The text as a woven fabric of course recalls R. Barthes' formulation of the narrative codes in *S/Z*.

In fact her fascination with Italian mosaics produced a curious dream recorded in the *Histoire de ma vie,* in which she projected her desire to create in the meticulous fashion of the artisan-worker, "je rêvais que je devenais mosaïste et je comptais attentivement mes petits carrés." (2: 206).[7] Although the world represented in *Les Maîtres mosaïstes* is primarily a male one, this novel clearly suggests feminist issues with which she deals more directly elsewhere. The narrator, even in this text, tends to deconstruct and repudiate traditional oppositions between masculine and feminine behavior (Valerio nurses his brother to health), high and low art (painting versus the craft of mosaic making), the artisanal work often attributed to women as opposed to male artistic creativity and genius. Sand produced relatively few essays about "high art" or the great painters of the Western tradition. Her close friendship with Delacroix, however, undoubtedly deepened her appreciation of painting; she wrote enthusiastically about his work in her autobiography, but also about Ingres and the remarkable purity of his line in *Questions d'art et de littérature* (65-71). In her discussions of artists she always stresses the importance of patient work, technique, and acute observation of exterior reality. Her sensitive portrait in *Histoire de ma vie* of Balzac's genius (2: 133-147) is based on the concept of energy and the enormous capacity for work he displayed.

There is even an important autobiographical aspect to *Les Maîtres mosaïstes.* One of Sand's most thoughtful essays on artist figures is devoted to a comparison of the techniques of Calamatta, the engraver, and Ingres.[8] In a letter addressed to her friend Calamatta (whose daughter married her beloved son Maurice), she explains that the Zuccati brothers are indeed patterned after Calamatta (Valerio) and his associate, Mercieri (Francesco) (*Correspondance* 2: 81). She claims that Calamatta had recreated a superb version of Ingres' famous painting "Le Voeu de Louis XII." Sand indeed considers this painting to be the religious masterpiece of her time, because of the precision of its contours and its profound emotional content (not many critics today would agree with her opinion of its

---

[7] This text is quoted by L'Hôpital in her discussion of *Les Maîtres mosaïstes* (168).

[8] The essay, entitled "Ingres et Calamatta," presents a subtle comparison of the techniques of painter and engraver (*Questions d'art et de littérature,* 65-71).

expressivity). Her comments suggest an ekphrastic analogy, or four-part homology, between the engraver and Ingres' work, and the Zuccati brothers who reproduced Titian's paintings. Calamatta, the engraver, must struggle with difficult, resistant materials in order to transpose an existing model into a beautiful object, just as the mosaic maker recreates the painter's cartoon through the laborious combination and application of precious stone and enamel.

I believe that Sand considered herself to be the imaginative artisan of the novel; she never wanted simply to reproduce the reality of the outside world in mimetic, realistic fashion. Her plots were sometimes linked to the Gothic tradition of fantastic or supernatural events (e.g., *La Comtesse de Rudolfstadt*, *La Mare au diable*), and her characters in the pastoral novels are often developed into idealized portraits of peasant folk from regional legends (*Les Maîtres sonneurs*). Even when based on actual political events and social situations, the basic data or model are transformed into an idealistic, novelistic creation through the innovative use of techniques like multi-voiced narration and point of view, linguistic experimentation, and the embodiment of ideas in fictional structures. Her novels, like the multi-colored mosaics she admired, embellish and heighten the realistic referent at their source.

Les Maîtres mosaïstes is clearly based on an historical model, namely the description of the trial of the Zuccati brothers found in the Venetian archives. Through poetic description of place, and especially the use of color imagery, Sand transforms the historical facts into an artistic representation of an idea–the already nostalgic ideal of a community or guild of artisan-artists cooperating to produce beautiful images of spiritual truths. In her notice to the edition of 1852 she explains her intention, using the humble metaphor of sewing on ornaments: "...je pris un fait réel dans l'histoire de l'art. Les aventures des mosaïstes de Saint-Marc sont vraies en grande partie. Je n'y ai cousu que quelques ornements, et j'ai développé des caractères que le fait même indique d'une manière assez certaine" (1).

The creator linked to the worker, or the worker-artist, is in effect Sand's ideal. The notion of the Renaissance guild had been revived in the current socialist theories of the phalanstery or commune in the works of Fourier. Pierre Leroux, who became her mentor in the years following their meeting in 1835, was the leading exponent of a form of socialist thought derived primarily from Saint-Simon that emphasized the valorization of the peasant and working classes. During the years of their close association she claimed that Leroux was her philosophical "savior," and she adopted his egalitarian theory of the necessary fusion of the classes through economic and political reform. His influence is clearly discernible in this novel which offers a portrait of artists and artisans struggling to achieve solidarity.

Sand's aesthetic of the novel is therefore realist-idealist; the novelist is a creative artisan of reality, and this is particularly true of the woman writer. Throughout her career Sand was suspicious of the dominant, male, romantic discourse concerning the genius figure, who is always represented as a man. She nevertheless expressed appreciation for the greatness of writers like Balzac, and even Hugo, who repeatedly proclaimed the prophetic, sacred nature of the male artist in poems like "La Mission du poète" and "Les Mages."

In many texts she presents the artistic temperament as essentially mysterious in origin, and art itself as inferior to the creativity of nature. Madeleine L'Hôpital, in her detailed study *La Notion d'artiste chez George Sand*, examined the many aspects of Sand's understanding of the artist figure, only to conclude that she was not a profound theorist in aesthetics. I would rather claim that she avoided intricate, philosophical or esoteric notions about art, because she strongly believed that creativity depends on craft, technique and community. She was, of course, acutely aware of the inferior position in which women artists had always been placed in the Western tradition. She knew that they were still excluded by the romantic metaphysics of creativity viewed primarily as a divine gift to men.

The beautiful ornaments or artistic heightening of *Les Maîtres mosaïstes* result from an effort to recapture some of the atmosphere or "local color" of late sixteenth-century Venice in words analogous to the sparkling pieces of mosaic she admired. There is little precise description of life in the city to be found, and few examples of ekphrasis or transpositions of actual artworks into the text. Sand does make, however, a very conscious use of pictorial language, and especially color symbolism that often raises the text to a poetic level.

The importance of intense color values in Venetian art is emphasized throughout the novel. Mosaics are prized because historically they preserve the warmth and richness of the painter's color scheme, and the unique quality of Venetian light, far longer and better than the paintings themselves. Sand's narrator suggests that the special light of Venice in its shimmering, watery landscape naturally evokes the colorful stones used by the mosaic makers. Titian, in his final appearance in the novel, justifies the special artistry of the Zuccati brothers by praising their exquisite use of color as well as their profound knowledge of design and composition.

Early in the text the narrator explains the technique used by the brothers to create the figures of the archangels in the central vault of the Basilica. She stresses "la science avec laquelle les Zuccati travaillaient en maîtres d'après les maîtres, traçaient eux-mêmes le dessin élégant et pur de leurs sujets, et créaient leur merveilleuse couleur d'après la simple indication du peintre" (22).

The major example of Sand's effort to transpose the special light and atmosphere of Venice into colorfully symbolic language is found in her description of the annual festival of St. Mark. The various guilds of artists and artisans parade through the Rialto dressed in the lively, unusual costumes characteristic of their corporation. The festival occurs at a culminating moment in the plot; Valerio, the sensualist, leads the procession of his company of the lizard, while his melancholy brother, Francesco, is languishing nearby in a gloomy prison. Sand skillfully contrasts the colorful pageantry of the festival with the tragic consequences of the repressive political regime. In fact her socialist viewpoint is discreetly present as her narrator observes that the joyous procession of workers and artists represents a false or artificial fusion of the classes in a society called a republic, but still dominated by a tyrannical, aristocratic oligarchy.

Although she later declared herself a "communist" (in the pre-Marxist sense) during the Revolution of 1848, she always proclaimed the need and possibility of a melding or fusion of the classes as opposed to a Marxist struggle–an opinion that many of her critics held to be naive. Leroux explained to Sand that the term "communionism" was preferable to the term "communism" since it was more faithful to their shared views on social reform. Her stance, however, can be understood in terms of her family background as well as a result of the profound influence of her friend and mentor. Her many efforts to mediate between the aristocratic grandmother who raised her and the proletarian mother whose absence caused her to suffer, help to explain her ideological advocacy of reconciliation. Her tendency to idealize peasant life and elevate that of the worker and artisan can therefore be appreciated also from an autobiographical perspective. Leroux, who was the major contemporary representative of socialist thought, after Fourier and before Proudhon, strongly advocated a peaceful melding of social classes through economic reform to form a new political unity.

Valerio leads the company of the lizard named for the reptile that clings to rooftops like the mosaic makers. Its members "portaient, comme leur chef, le pourpoint vert et le reste de l'habillement blanc, collant; mais ils avaient le pourpoint de dessous en soie jaune, la plume écarlate, et l'écusson noir et argent." (134). The lengthy passage describing the festival is rich with precise notations of color such as these; and even more interestingly, it constitutes an attempt to suggest the atmosphere of the scene through a harmonious color scheme very much like that of the mosaics themselves.

In the following passage Sand comes very close to what Gautier would term a "transposition d'art"–an ekphrastic effort to transform a mosaic into text. She describes the decoration of Valerio's horse in terms of a kind of mosaic pattern dominated by objects of white and silver with highlights of red:

> Le seul Valerio, soumis aux lois d'un goût plus pur, parut sur un cheval turc *blanc* comme *la neige*, et d'une beauté remarquable. Il n'avait qu'une simple housse de peau de tigre, et de grandes *bandelettes d'argent* lui servaient de rênes; ses crins, longs et soyeux, mêlés à des *fils d'argent*, étaient tressés, et chaque tresse se terminait par une belle *fleur de grenade* en *argent ciselé*, d'un travail exquis. Ses sabots, et sa queue, abondante et magnifique, battait librement ses flancs généreux. Il avait, comme son maître, le lézard *d'argent* sur *fond cramoisi*, peint avec un soin extrême sur la cuisse gauche. (136; emphasis mine)

Annarosa Poli, in her study of the influence of Italy on Sand's work, claims that in March of 1834 Sand had witnessed a procession in front of Saint Mark's similar to the one she describes in *Les Maîtres mosaïstes* (180). Poli also suggests that Giovanni Bellini's famous painting of Corpus Christi Day in the Piazza, found in the Accademia in Venice, might be another source for Sand's representation of the festival. In any case we know from her correspondence that Sand often used the costumes she had observed in paintings of Titian and Tintoretto as models for her descriptions in the "Italian" novels and short stories.

In violent contrast to the elegant beauty of the figures in the festival whose sign is silver, the gloomy dungeon where Francesco is incarcerated is described through fiery, red images suggesting suffering and death:

> le soleil inexorable se couchait dans une mer de feu, et teignait d'un reflet sinistre ces murs peints en rouge, qui semblent absorber et conserver sans relâche l'ardeur de l'incendie. La peste étendait de plus en plus ses ravages. Tous les bruits animés et joyeux de la brillante Venise avaient fait place à un silence de mort, interrompu seulement par les lugubres sons de la cloche des agonisants, et par les lointaines psalmodies de quelque moine pieux qui passait sur le canal, conduisant au cimetière une barque pleine de cadavres. (160-161)

Sand introduces the theme of death in Venice with an emphasis on the resurgence of the plague during the last years of the 16th century. The epidemic becomes a visible sign of the injustice of the inquisition, and the tyranny of the corrupt government responsible for Francesco's suffering. In the above passage the use of color (the sinister, fiery red reflections) is complemented by the lugubrious music of the death-knell and the chants of the monks. The narrator creates aural as well as color sensations to produce in the reader a sentiment of the palpable presence of death in the city.

Les Maîtres mosaïstes is an unjustly neglected, elegantly written, and poetic reconstruction of an important aspect of the artist's life in late Renaissance Venice. The novel is also a rich and valuable representation of Sand's aesthetic concepts; the precision and artistry of mosaic making suggest an apt metaphor for the complex patterning of words and images that compose a text. This fictional account of real events eloquently expresses her utopian dream for the artist whose sense of craft and community constitutes his real genius. After enduring a very romantic rite of passage from spiritual death to rebirth, the artisan brothers who are restoring the great mosaics of the medieval and Byzantine past succeed in affirming their individual worth as artists while together they serve a common religious ideal.

CHAPTER 4

PAINTING AS INTERTEXT IN BALZAC'S
LA FILLE AUX YEUX D'OR

*L*A *Duchesse de Langeais* and *La Fille aux yeux d'or* are dedicated respectively to Liszt and Delacroix. These two novels, from the trilogy *L'Histoire des Treize*, can be considered experimental novels in which Balzac shows his skill at developing interartistic parallels as musician and painter. *La Duchesse* includes a conscious attempt to reproduce musical structures in fiction; *La Fille aux yeux d'or* is almost a romantic "transposition d'art." Balzac endeavors to produce aesthetic effects similar to those of Delacroix's paintings: a strange beauty elicited by images of violent passion. Through the use of pictorial description, color symbolism, and structural devices related to painting, he creates exotic "oriental" scenes in the midst of modern Paris, calculated to rival works like Hugo's *Orientales* and Delacroix's *La Mort de Sardanapale*.

Olivier Bonard has studied the role of painting in Balzac's early works, including *Le Père Goriot*.[1] He finds specific paintings (real or imagined) to be the point of departure of the narrative in texts like *La Maison du chat-qui-pelote*, *Sarrazine* and *Le Chef-d'oeuvre inconnu*. Characters and narrative situations develop from a picture named and described rather than from "realistic" or "objective" social observation. Examples are Girodet's *Endymion* for *Sarrazine*, Gros's *La Bataille d'Eylau* for *Le Colonel Chabert*, and the Flemish realists for other works. Balzac's narrator, for example, introduces Paquita Valdès, the girl with the golden eyes, as the incarnation of a

---

[1] A partial refutation of Bonard's book is found in Jean-Loup Bourget's article, "Balzac et le pictural."

figure from an ancient vase painting, the woman caressing her chimera. Georges Hirschell has minutely examined the personal and artistic relations between Balzac and Delacroix, as well as the color symbolism found in Delacroix's paintings and its analog in Balzac's stylistic devices in *La Fille aux yeux d'or*.

This chapter attempts to analyze the function of Delacroix's paintings as intertexts: the ways in which specific paintings give structure and suggest meaning to the novel, and the narrative techniques used by Balzac that are apparently borrowed from painting, and, more specifically, from Delacroix's works. Any discussion of the intertextuality of painting in this novel must first examine the entire pattern of intertextual references that might appear to the casual reader to be unnecessarily copious and even contradictory.

Balzac's famous description of Paris as hell, in which he compares the spherical social structure of the city to the circles of Dante's *Inferno*, provides the novel with its organizing principle. A city dominated by "l'or et le plaisir" whose ascending movement from proletariat to aristocracy is degraded by the relentless pursuit of money is the setting for the tragic, corrupted love of Paquita, Henri de Marsay, and his sister, Euphémie. In a hellish city dominated by degraded values, in which human energy and potential are wasted in the pursuit of money and sensual pleasure, life without a spiritual dimension produces a hellish love.

The role of Dante's *Inferno* as intertext is, however, more subtle and complex than has been established by previous critics. Balzac's narrator mentions only four circles of hell, or five, if we include the place of the artists. He does not mention the seventh circle in which are found those who have betrayed loved ones. Francesca da Rimini, who deceived her husband in favor of his brother, was relegated to this outer circle, and her story must be considered the original model of the triangle in this novel. Paquita betrays her lover, Euphémie, in favor of Euphémie's brother, Henri de Marsay, thus creating an ironic modern version of Dante's triangle. The circular unity of the novel is complete; the tragic conclusion of betrayal and murder brings the reader back to the beginning of the text. Paquita's story can be situated in the secret center of Paris as hell, where the city's violence and cruelty are paradoxically the most acute.

Balzac uses intertextual reference to literature and myth in order to lure the reader; he suggests a variety of possible interpretations in order to surprise and astonish him with the impact of the final scenes. Reference to Delacroix's paintings, however, arguably provides the reader with the clues required to make a more coherent and profound reading of *La Fille aux yeux d'or*.

Balzac's narrator compares his story to "une vieille comédie," referring specifically to the "Barbier de Séville." The reader is led to believe that De Marsay is struggling to attract the beautiful and innocent young Paquita away from the elderly gentleman who has raised and educated her for himself. The allusion to the plot of *L'Ecole des femmes*, with its traditional comic triangle, is reinforced by a reference to the myth of Pygmalion and Galatea. The exquisite Paquita seems to have been "created" for the special pleasure of an aging Marquis. A comic and cynical tone is thus maintained throughout most of the main section of the novel; but certain references disconcert the reader. The first meeting of the lovers is compared to a scene from a Gothic novel of Ann Radcliffe; its macabre setting hints at a tragic outcome. Paquita and her monstrous mother are compared to a "sirène" and her "chimère," suggesting the destructive illusions of love. Near the end of the novel, Sade's *Justine* and *Les Liaisons dangereuses* are invoked as textual signs of perversion and cruelty.

De Marsay is compared to Adonis, but also to a serpent from the lost paradise. He is likened to a lion and a centaur but also to Othello, suggesting jealousy and betrayal. In an effort to give the fiction a philosophical dimension, Balzac describes De Marsay as Don Juan, Manfred, and above all, as a new Faust who is seeking the absolute in the form of perfect feminine sensuality and beauty. The myth of Faust is the most resonant textual allusion, suggesting the deepest meanings of the fiction. De Marsay's quest for the absolute leads to death and destruction because he has placed his ideal in a degraded mode: the search for "l'or et le plaisir," infinite sensual pleasure without a spiritual dimension, becomes a hellish love in a hellish city.

With the Parisian dandy De Marsay as a modern Faust, the novel begins to resemble the series of *Etudes philosophiques* that Balzac was publishing at the same time. Each one (e.g. *La Peau de chagrin*) presented a variation on the theme of human energy engaged in a death struggle against the limitations imposed on man by his physical and temporal condition.

An examination of the meanings suggested by the numerous textual and mythological references (far from exhausted in this account) thus suggests that the basically comic plot of *La Fille* is gradually transformed into a tragic one. Figaro is transformed into Faust, and the traditional love triangle is inverted to produce an almost Greek-like family tragedy replete with suggestions of incest and homosexuality.[2]

Delacroix's well-known work *Femmes d'Alger dans leur appartement* (1834), painted the same year as *La Fille* was published, and *La Mort de Sardanapale* (1828) are the specific paintings that play the role of intertext in this novel. Various sketches and paintings of animals being hunted or attacked by other animals, done even before Delacroix's trip to Morocco, are also represented in the fiction. In his lengthy prologue to the action of the novel, Balzac's narrator refers to the "petites peuplades heureuses qui vivent à l'orientale" (5: 1053), enclaves of beautiful women who somehow escape from the corrupting economic and social dynamics of the city to live in an intimate feminine refuge. In preserving their beauty they constitute an exception to the general degradation of the Parisian people that Balzac has described in caricatural detail in the first pages of his novel. Paquita's hotel is closed like an oriental harem, and she, the captive woman, is characterized as a veritable seraglio of pleasure. Certainly aware of Delacroix's trip to North Africa, Balzac suggests that it is not necessary to leave Paris to find scenes of extravagant luxury and sensuous beauty. He seems to intend his carefully composed descriptions of Paquita's boudoir to rival Delacroix's depiction of the exotic setting of the Algerian women.

The scenes in the harem-like atmosphere of the secret bedrooms are presented through the narrative distance of "scènes-tableaux." This technique of pictorial description in which a scene is composed as if it were already a painting is characteristic of much romantic writing from Chateaubriand to Flaubert's *Madame Bovary*. Balzac uses a painter's antithesis and violent contrast to distinguish between the first setting of the lovers' meeting, a sordid room resembling an abandoned bordello, dominated by harsh reds, greens, and yellows, and the elegant gilded boudoir where the lovers finally consumate their passion.

---

[2] Shoshanna Felman has subtly analyzed the novel's complex psychological significance for the modern reader in "Rereading Femininity."

The second boudoir scene, elaborately detailed, is the best example of Balzac's particular kind of "transposition d'art." It illustrates his techniques with a virtuoso richness surpassing any similar attempts in his other novels.[3] Lines, contours and forms are presented with an almost geometric precision; half the boudoir "décrivait une ligne circulaire mollement gracieuse, qui s'opposait à l'autre partie parfaitement carrée" (5: 1087). Curved and straight lines thus function as signifiers of the feminine and masculine principles that will confront each other here. In the ensuing description the forms are repeated and reinforced. The horseshoe curved frame behind the immense Turkish bed is surmounted by a red tapestry decorated with Indian muslin "cannelée comme l'est une colonne corinthienne" (5: 1088). The effect of straight columns is achieved by "des tuyaux alternativement creux et ronds" molded into the cloth upon which were designed the curved lines of "des arabesques noires" (5: 1088). The repetition and interplay of these forms suggests the careful composition of a painting and serves also as a signifying code for the lovers' encounter. Balzac pays close attention to the spatial arrangement of objects, and the source of light that illuminates their oriental richness is carefully indicated: "Le plafond, au milieu duquel pendait un lustre en vermeil mat, étincelait de blancheur, et la corniche était dorée" (5: 1088). The point of view throughout the scene is that of the observer De Marsay who is aware that every element of the "tableau" has been calculated to produce desire.

The narrator indicates the play of light and shadow that seems to reproduce certain shimmering effects (almost pre-impressionist) of Delacroix's color scheme: "Les chatoiements de la tenture, dont la couleur changeait suivant la direction du regard, en devenant ou toute blanche, ou toute rose, s'accordaient avec les effets de la lumière qui s'infusait dans les diaphanes tuyaux de la mousseline, en produisant de nuageuses apparences" (5: 1088). Balzac insists above all on a pattern of color that dominates the composition, giving it its form and possible meanings. A prevalent scheme of white, gold, and red is established in the objects and flowers of the

---

[3] The description of Frenhofer's studio, for example, in *Le Chef-d'oeuvre inconnu*, which is calculated to evoke the same effects as Rembrandt's chiaroscuro, or the realistic Flemish painting by Sommervieux in *La Maison du chat-qui-pelote*.

boudoir and intensified almost to excess through the repetition of words indicating the presence of these colors and their variants, "rose," "ponceau." The word "rouge" is used nine times in a single paragraph, as if Balzac considered the repetition to constitute a series of "taches" or brush strokes on the canvas. Although Balzac attempts to focalize on De Marsay as a direct witness of this "scène-tableau," his narrator interprets the color symbolism; he concludes the description with the kind of musical metaphor that Baudelaire will later apply to the paintings of Delacroix: "Il y avait dans cette harmonie parfaite un concert de couleurs auquel l'âme répondait par des idées voluptueuses, indécises, flottantes" (5: 1088).

There is thus a profound correspondence between color and human desire; the highly colored pictorial impression of the boudoir is intended to suggest unexpressed or even inexpressible needs and desires. In Balzac's view, the language of color is perhaps superior to that of words because its meanings are less restricted by conventional signifieds or denotations. Balzac's narrator concludes:

> L'âme a je ne sais quel attachement pour le blanc, l'amour se plaît dans le rouge, et l'or flatte les passions, il a la puissance de réaliser leurs fantaisies. Ainsi tout ce que l'homme a de vague et de mystérieux en lui-même, toutes ses affinités inexpliquées se trouvaient caressées dans leurs sympathies involontaires. (5: 1088)

The dominant color pattern—white, red, and gold—can therefore correspond to ideas and evoke qualities and desires both physical and spiritual. Colors as signifiers can attach themselves to multiple signifieds, thus producing complex, ambiguous signs, and potentially even expressing the concealed inner world of the reader. When this boudoir scene is considered in the context of the entire novel, it is clear once again that its meanings are ambivalent. White stands for purity, red for love, and gold flatters the passions. The narrator, however, has neglected to analyze the fourth color in the scheme, named five times in the same passage—black. The vivid presence of black is certainly intended to foreshadow death and the tragedy to come. The reader will also soon discover that red connotes blood as well as passion and that gold signals corruption.

The predominance of red, often identified with Delacroix's coloristic innovations, thus suggests the ambiguity at the center of the text. Red signifies passion *and* blood; or rather, passion is blood because "la volupté mène à la férocité" (5: 1097), as Balzac's narrator will declare in the stated moral of the fiction. Sexuality and sensuality are inextricably linked to violence and cruelty in a world without spiritual values, where white suggests only an illusion of purity (Paquita is deceived but she is not innocent), and gold represents the degraded economic value of money as well as men's fantasies of fortune.

The pictorial description of the boudoir reveals the hidden meanings of the text to the reader contemplating the "tableau." The conflict between the sexes is encoded in the formal pattern of objects, and the color scheme suggests major themes common to Balzac's fiction and to Delacroix's painting. First there is an exotic captive woman in a golden oriental setting, and then, sumptuous objects of rich color evoking sensual passion, and finally, the potential for violence and cruelty. At the end of the description of the boudoir, the narrator can convincingly introduce Paquita as "le chef-d'oeuvre de la création" (5: 1089), whose complexion is "chaudement coloré," her beautiful skin "dorée par les reflets du rouge et par l'effusion de je ne sais quelle vapeur d'amour" (5: 1089).

Although *Femmes d'Alger dans leur appartement* is arguably the intertext for the boudoir scenes in the novel, one cannot claim that Balzac is "imitating" the painting. The composition of Balzac's "scène-tableau" clearly differs from that of the picture (architectural details are not as prominent in the painting, and a group of women is present); and Balzac's color scheme is far more contrastive than the muted, warm tones of Delacroix's *Femmes d'Alger*. The color scheme that Balzac proposes–variations of white, red, gold, and black–corresponds more specifically to *La Mort de Sardanapale*, the other major "transposed" painting in the novel. Just as *Femmes d'Alger* situates and explains the role of Paquita, *La Mort de Sardanapale* functions to develop the psychology of Henri de Marsay and gives him a legendary, archetypal resonance. Elements of this great painting are reproduced not by a specific scene, but by a series of allusions–themes, characters, metaphors–suggesting the importance of this intertextual reference.

During the melancholy initial encounter between De Marsay and Paquita, Balzac begins transforming his superficial Parisian dandy into a splendid and disenchanted romantic hero. Totally bored with the facile pleasures of the city, he is "affamé de voluptés nouvelles," and compared to "ce roi d'orient qui demandait qu'on lui créât un plaisir, soif horrible dont les grandes âmes sont saisies" (5: 1082). The ideal beauty of Paquita becomes in his imagination "l'infini rendu palpable" (5: 1082); his desire to possess her is presented as a Faustian quest for an absolute that alone would give Henri's existence a meaning.

According to the legend of Sardanapalus, the Assyrian despot realized the futility of defending his lands against invading hordes and ordered that his goods, his servants, and his women be burned with him on a funeral pyre. The legend was reinterpreted by the romantics,[4] especially Byron, Delacroix, and even Berlioz who found in it a contemporary image of despair or "mal du siècle." As seen by the romantics, Sardanapalus is overcome with spleen before the tragic imperfections and limitations of the real world and dreams of pleasures and beauty beyond the mediocrity of existence. In spite of his power and great wealth, he chooses death and creates an extraordinary spectacle of destruction that for a moment at least will relieve him from a paralyzing boredom. Like Baudelaire's poet-narrator in "Au lecteur" and "Le Voyage," prelude and conclusion to *Les Fleurs du mal*, he dreams of death in order to find "du nouveau."[5]

Allusions to Sardanapalus and to aspects of Delacroix's painting that reinforce this reading of the legend are repeated throughout the rest of Balzac's text. During the initial encounter with Henri, Paquita is already seen as his potential victim, "absorbée comme une femme faible devant la hache du bourreau et tuée d'avance par une crainte..." (5: 1081). This phrase suggests the scene of carnage

---

[4] Jack J. Spector discusses the sources for Delacroix's painting as well as Byronic romanticism and the psychological background in general in *Delacroix: The Death of Sardanapalus*. Byron's play *Sardanapalus* (1821) impressed the French romantics including Berlioz, who composed a cantata on the subject in 1831, entitled *La dernière nuit de Sardanapale*.

[5] It has been suggested that Baudelaire's introductory poem was, in part, inspired by Delacroix's painting. "Au lecteur" presents the portrait of those whose corrosive "ennui" leads to dreams of violence and destruction: "Il ferait volontiers de la terre un débris / Et dans un baillement avalerait le monde."

in the foreground of Delacroix's painting, especially the beautiful female figure who has abandoned herself to the King's assassin. De Marsay is described by the narrator as a man of great energy whose potential strength has been stimulated by his sexual desire for Paquita. Confidence in his sexuality appears to lead him to a sense of extraordinary power: "De Marsay exerçait le pouvoir autocratique du despote oriental" who "pouvait ce qu'il voulait dans l'intérêt de ses plaisirs et de ses vanités. Cette invisible action sur le monde social l'avait revêtu d'une majesté réelle" (5: 1084-85). Endowed now with a "conscience léonine" (5: 1085), De Marsay's character is magnified and generalized by the narrator who gives him a mythical dimension:

> Les femmes aiment prodigieusement ces gens qui se nomment pachas eux-mêmes, qui semblent accompagnés de lions, de bourreaux, et marchent dans un appareil de terreur. Il en résulte chez ces hommes une sécurité d'action, une certitude de pouvoir, une fierté de regard, une conscience léonine qui réalise pour les femmes le type de force qu'elles rêvent toutes. Ainsi était de Marsay. (5: 1085)

There is an obvious link between eroticism and death in Delacroix's painting, which made it disturbing to contemporary viewers. The sadistic killing of beautiful women on the immense bed of an indifferent king was a forceful and disturbing subject for a salon painting in 1828.[6] Balzac understood, surely, the essential message of the picture, and in a series of boudoir scenes he, too, presents sexuality as a violently aggressive act. The final encounter between Paquita and De Marsay's sister, in which Paquita is brutally murdered, the red of her blood spattering the white furnishings of the secret room, is calculated to disturb the reader as much as the *Sardanapale* was intended to shock the contemporary viewer.

In the third of the four boudoir scenes, when Paquita dresses Henri as a woman and calls him "Mariquita," thus emasculating him and suggesting his impotence, a violent struggle to the death occurs between the two lovers. This love-death combat is abruptly ended, however, by the faithful servant, Christemio the Moor. His

---

[6] Spector analyzes the painting as a projection of Delacroix's own sadistic sexual fantasies and situates it in the context of romantic imagery.

powerful figure seems to echo the imposing presence of the Moor in the foreground of Delacroix's painting where he is both assassin and doomed slave. Ironically, this confrontation foreshadows the final love-death scene of the two women that Balzac's narrator will compare to a violent combat between two animals.

Both scenes contain several allusions to *La Mort de Sardanapale* and also to the numerous sketches and paintings of animal hunts that Delacroix painted throughout his career.[7] The frightened horse, which is being led to the funeral pyre in the left part of the foreground in the *Sardanapale*, is a constant motif in Delacroix's works. The figure of the strong animal, horse, lion, or tiger, as a symbol of energy and passion falling victim to fate, is echoed by Balzac's numerous animal metaphors in the novel. De Marsay is often compared to animals of strength and prowess–lions, tigers, eagles–but also to animals with more negative connotations: he is clever as a monkey and resembles the serpent in a garden. Paquita is compared to a cat, her duenna to a hyena, and Christemio to a bird of prey. The animal imagery contributes to the "oriental" exoticism of the text and signals, as it does in most romantic writing, the baser nature of the Parisian lovers. When De Marsay is outraged by suspicion of Paquita's motives, the narrator declares: "il laissa éclater le rugissement du tigre dont une gazelle se serait moquée, le cri d'un tigre qui joignait à la force de la bête l'intelligence du démon" (5: 1096). The image of a tiger pursuing a gazelle accurately characterizes the plot of this novel, and evokes the cruel ironies of Delacroix's dramatic animal sketches in which he so masterfully portrays the tragic fate of the trapped animal.

In the final boudoir scene, De Marsay's sister brutally murders Paquita, whose body is "déchiqueté à coups de poignard" (5: 1107). Balzac represents the bloody end of the struggle through the eyes of De Marsay, who has arrived too late to prevent it. His sister has replaced the "bourreau" of Delacroix's painting; Balzac's narra-

---

[7] Delacroix painted most of his scenes of lion and tiger hunts after his trip to North Africa in 1832, thus after the publication of *La Fille aux yeux d'or* (1834). Under the influence of Géricault and George Stubbs, however, he had already produced violent drawings of animals, especially horses during the 1820's. Balzac was probably acquainted with some of these works, such as the lithographs of the "Wild Horse" and the "Horse attacked by a Tiger" (1828), now in the Metropolitan Museum of Art, New York.

tor describes her as "sublime" when transported by an ecstasy of violence. Although covered with blood and bleeding herself,

> Sa tête avide et furieuse respirait l'odeur du sang. Sa bouche haletante restait entrouverte, et ses narines ne suffisaient pas à ses aspirations. Certains animaux, mis en fureur, fondent sur leur ennemi, le mettent à mort, et, tranquilles dans leur victoire, semblent avoir tout oublié. Il en est d'autres, qui tournent autour de leur victime, qui la gardent en craignant qu'on ne la leur vienne enlever... (5: 1107)

The irony of this final scene is enriched by reference to Delacroix's *Sardanapale*. De Marsay is a passive witness to the brutal murder that he has provoked. The act is committed not by Delacroix's moor (or Christemio in the novel), but by De Marsay's sister, thus emphasizing his own impotence. The paradox of the painting underlies that of the novel as well: De Marsay's apparent strength, his "leonine" prowess, conceals a profound weakness. Sardanapalus organized an elaborate suicide when confronted with the powerlessness of his situation. De Marsay does not even succeed in taking the "manly" vengeance he had planned on Paquita for her having betrayed him. By murdering her, his feminine double eliminates the sign of his weakness; his sister's sadistic love had a force he could never produce. This bloody, "oriental" denouement does indeed evoke the violence of a Delacroix animal hunt, and suggest Baudelaire's attraction for the beauty of evil. Not only does Balzac's narrator compare Euphémie (in her bloodthirst) to a ferocious animal; she is also like Homer's Achilles, who insisted on dragging his dead enemy nine times around Troy. Balzac admires the grandeur of her crime just as Baudelaire cites the strange beauty of extravagant criminal acts in the opening poem of *Les Fleurs du mal*.

The Parisian comedy has become a Greek tragedy of betrayal and vengeance acted out more or less "en famille." After the murder, Euphémie takes final leave of her brother, whom she resembles both physically and morally: "Adieu, dit-elle, rien ne console d'avoir perdu ce qui nous a paru être l'infini" (5: 1109). Her words point to the deepest level of the tragedy in the context Balzac has created. De Marsay and his sister have placed the quest for the absolute in a degraded mode. The desire for an infinite of physical pleasure and beauty has replaced the quest for spiritual wisdom, artistic perfection, or scientific knowledge, those worthy goals of Balzac's protagonists in the *Etudes philosophiques*. Before the tragic end, the narrator has already characterized De Marsay as a modern Faust with the sexual drives of a Don Juan:

> il trouva dans *la Fille aux yeux d'or* ce sérail que sait créer la femme aimante et à laquelle un homme ne renonce jamais. Paquita répondait à cette passion que sentent tous les hommes vraiment grands pour l'infini, passion mystérieuse si dramatiquement exprimée dans Faust, si poétiquement traduite dans Manfred, et qui poussait Don Juan à fouiller le coeur des femmes, en espérant y trouver cette pensée sans bornes à la recherche de laquelle se mettent tant de chasseurs de spectres, que les savants croient entrevoir dans la science, que les mystiques trouvent en Dieu seul. L'espérance d'avoir enfin l'Etre idéal avec lequel la lutte pouvait être constante sans fatigue, ravit de Marsay qui, pour la première fois, depuis longtemps, ouvrit son coeur. (5: 1101)

De Marsay's particular kind of "mal du siècle" can largely be explained in *La Fille aux yeux d'or* by the corrupting influence of the modern city. The organizing principle of the text, "l'or et le plaisir" (as the narrator states in the prologue), determines De Marsay as well as the Parisians for whom he seems to be an exception. Paquita is both "or" and "plaisir" for him; the goal of his quest is not spiritual love but the inexhaustible riches of sensuality. His search is profoundly materialistic, and the luxury of the dandy's self-created image is the tool of seduction. Balzac's De Marsay is the necessary product of a city whose degraded values, money and pleasure, have replaced an authentic spiritual life. The "hellish" loves of De Marsay and his sister for the golden victim are played out not in an oriental harem but in the hell of modern Paris, where human energy is perverted and dissipated in the economic spiral of social mobility.

Balzac's rich and complex use of color imagery is found throughout the text and constitutes a kind of tribute to Delacroix, whose painting was both praised and criticized for its innovative color schemes. The color red, associated particularly with Delacroix, is an ambiguous sign in the novel and situated at the center of its meanings, a symbol of passion, blood, and suffering. Gold is also laden with multiple meanings: it represents the mysterious richness promised by Paquita's eyes, oriental sensuality, and the supreme value of modern Paris. It is an ambiguous sign, connoting pleasure as well as money and moral decay. Balzac utilizes strong color contrasts and the dramatic play of light and darkness, also important elements of Delacroix's technique. Paquita's golden richness is contrasted with the dark (noire) beauty of De Marsay's sister. In spite of her brilliance, Paquita has lived in the darkness (les ténèbres) waiting for the light (lumière) Henri can bring.

A special use of color is also found in the Prologue of the novel to describe the city and its hierarchical spiral of inhabitants. Although the novel is appropriately dedicated to Delacroix, the prologue more clearly suggests Daumier, who was the real painter of Parisian life during the years of the July Monarchy. Rather than the bright colors associated with Delacroix's paintings, Balzac's narrator uses grays, blue, and brown to caricature his Parisians. The Parisian face has become "grise comme le plâtre des maisons" (5: 1040), and the unique struggle for money "décolore, blêmit, bleuit, et brunit plus ou moins les individus" (1040). Dominated by the profound materialism of his life, the Parisian's physiognomy reveals a "teinte presque infernale" (5: 1039). The populace is a "peuple horrible à voir, hâve, jaune, tanné" (5: 1039). Balzac repeats colors, or verbs suggesting color, to evoke brush strokes or a dominant color scheme on the canvas. Thus, the worker in the outer circle of hell who expends his energy in the preparation of objects for the rich:

> dore les porcelaines, coud les habits et les robes, amincit le fer, amenuise le bois, tisse l'acier, solidifie le chanvre et le fil, satine les bronzes, festonne le cristal, imite les fleurs, brode la laine, dresse les chevaux, tresse les harnais et les galons, découpe le cuivre, peint les voitures, arrondit les vieux ormeaux, vaporise le coton, souffle les tuls, corrode le diamant, polit les métaux, transforme en feuilles le marbre, lèche les cailloux, toilette la pensée, colore, blanchit et noircit tout. (5: 1041)

In the Prologue, activities are enumerated, color symbols superabound, and verbs of action and color seem self-generating. This verbal excess can even suggest the harsh dark lines in a Daumier caricature. When he takes his pleasure, for example, the worker does so in a "lassante débauche brune de peau, noire de tapes, blême d'ivresse, ou jaune d'indigestion..." (5: 1041). For each class in the social spiral, Balzac creates a caricature, a generalized portrait of its typical representatives, emphasizing with comic intensity the negative effects of social and economic pressure. The petit bourgeois "persiste à vivre et vit, mais crétinisé: vous le rencontrez à face usée, plate, vieille, sans lueur aux yeux, sans fermeté dans la jambe, se traînant d'un air hébété sur le boulevard" (5: 1045). Balzac's harshest picture is reserved for the grand bourgeois, lawyer, doctor, or judge, the major subjects of Daumier's cartoons: "leurs figures s'arrondissent, s'aplatissent, se rougissent" (5: 1048). When they have achieved social standing "leurs figures offrent... cette pâleur aigre, ces colorations fausses, ses yeux ternis, cernés, ces bouches bavardes et sensuelles où l'observateur reconnaît les symptômes de l'abâtardissement de la pensée..." (5: 1048).

La Fille aux yeux d'or, like *La Duchesse de Langeais*, might be read as important prose experiments in the interrelation of the arts. Balzac attempted to create with words an effect and impact resembling those of painting–the negative force of Daumier's satirical drawings, or the exotic beauty of Delacroix's colored images of violence and passion. The use of "scènes-tableaux" forces the reader to be a viewer, to contemplate and "decode" the meanings found in the formal patterns. The scene transformed into a picture prepares for the drama to follow through a description of the décor, and contains a complex, constructed signifying system. Pictorial description, color symbolism and intertextual references to paintings and sketches are, in the last analysis, perhaps more important than the subject matter of the novel.

Seen in the context of nineteenth-century fascination with possible "correspondences," Balzac's "oriental" novel is a major contribution to the long and controversial history of interarts comparisons.[8] In spite of the fundamental limitations inherent in any

---

[8] Wendy Steiner's *The Colors of Rhetoric* begins with a detailed examination of the history of the interarts comparison from Antiquity to the present. It includes an illuminating structuralist analysis of William Carlos Williams's *Pictures from Breughel*.

attempt to transpose one medium into another, in this case fixed visual imagery into a narration evolving in time, *La Fille aux yeux d'or* is perhaps the best and most successful example of a romantic "transposition d'art" in novelistic form. It richly complements Hugo's exotic picture-poems in the *Orientales*, Delacroix's highly literary paintings and illustrations from Shakespeare and Faust, and Berlioz's many transcriptions of fictional works, including the regrettably lost music for the death of Sardanapalus.

CHAPTER 5

THE ART COLLECTION: AUTHENTIC VALUES IN BALZAC'S *LE COUSIN PONS*

BALZAC'S final novels *Les Parents pauvres* (1846-47) present a contrasting diptych concerning the marginalized cousins, Bette and Sylvain Pons. The first cousin succeeds in destroying the Hulot family (left over pseudo-aristocrats from the Empire) who had always disdained her; Pons, on the other hand, is finally driven to his death by his wealthy bourgeois relatives and their avaricious allies. His awkward and harmful efforts to help his family realize an advantageous marriage seal his fate.

From lawyers and doctors to the unforgettable concierge, La Cibot, human greed has rarely been portrayed so unremittingly. Both Bette and Pons are indeed "queer cousins" as well as poor relations with whom the narrator sympathizes. They live, nevertheless, outside the mainstream of society which, in order to perpetuate its values (money, social position), rejects them.[1] Bette's probable lesbian relationship with Valerie Marneff and Pons' sentimental union with the naive German musician, Schmucke, are evidence enough of their marginality. They seem to pose a serious threat to the narrator's (and Balzac's) conservative reliance on the traditional institutions of marriage and family, whose values have been undermined by the exaggerated individualism unleashed by the Revolution, and successive political upheavals.

Bette loses her beloved, young artist protégé, Steinbock, due to the treachery of her cousin Hortense; Pons, on the other hand, has amassed an amazing collection of artworks, that function as a kind

---

[1] See Michael Lucey's essay "Balzac's Queer Cousins and Their Friends."

of sublimation of erotic desire and a compensation for his failure as a composer.

The painting collection, showpiece of the 1,907 art objects in his apartment, is truly the heroine of the novel.[2] It represents not only Pons' extraordinary talent as collector, but as we shall see, Balzac's own version of an ideal private museum of Western painting. The cultural phenomenon of collecting seems to assume new importance at the end of the 18th century; Elgin's marbles and Napoleon's acquisitions during his military campaigns are often cited as influential political models. The concept of the museum itself as a public space for storing national treasures and displaying art is firmly established with the creation of the Louvre in Paris during the Revolutionary period. A case can even be made for *Le Cousin Pons* as the first major French novel to problematize the theme of the individual art collector.

Pons the collector, however, can be characterized as yet another "raté" in the long succession of nineteenth-century failed artist figures. As a young romantic he received the Prix de Rome for music in 1814; he never achieved great success in music composition, but began seriously to acquire artworks in Italy. Physically unattractive and flawed by the sin of gourmandise (the fault that precipitates his downfall), he becomes one of Balzac's strongest representatives of obsessive behavior carried to the extreme of monomania: "une manie, c'est le plaisir passé à l'état d'idée" (5: 168).

Obsessive collecting of art becomes his raison d'être, sublimating his desire for women into the great beauty of masterworks, and replacing his original creative impulse in music. Although he becomes a victim of a society that disdains and eventually destroys him, his collection will ultimately represent the uneasy triumph of art in a materialistic world.

The authentic aesthetic values of art remain uncorrupted at the end of the novel, and the artworks are not transformed into com-

---

[2] The art collection has been the subject of several recent studies including John P. Greene's treatment of the collection as protagonist in "Balzac's Most Helpless Heroine: The Art Collection in *Le Cousin Pons*." See also Eric Bordas, "Le Rôle de la peinture dans *Le Cousin Pons*." Balzac's early novel *La Peau de chagrin* (1831), part of the *Etudes philosophiques*, presents a dealer in antiquities, and the art dealer Elie Magus is a recurring character in Balzac's *Comédie humaine*. It has also been suggested that a possible literary antecedent for Balzac's interest in the phenomenon of collecting can be found in Sir Walter Scott's novel *The Antiquary*, 1816.

modities, since the essential collection (minus several stolen works) becomes the property of the Comte Popinot. This upper-bourgeois relative, a kind of nineteenth-century Rockefeller or Getty, will preserve the artworks from the instability of the state and the insatiable greed of the other relatives, whose only concern is to profit from them as marketable objects. The text lends itself almost too readily to a Marxist interpretation.[3] The narrator's perspective, however, and the final effect of the novel suggest another possible reading. It is true that the devalorization of art in the new society dominated by the bourgeoisie is, indeed, made abundantly clear. Everyone except Pons, Magus (the art dealer) and Popinot treat the art object as no more than a commodity to be exchanged on the market. Paintings are replaced, sold, substituted for each other, and considered only for their monetary worth with no concern for their unique qualities.

Reactions to the two final testaments of Pons symbolize the current attitudes of the dominant class, but also demonstrate Balzac's rather unexpected, guarded optimism about the preservation of the authentic values of art in modern society. Pons' first testament decreed that his only friend Schmucke (their relationship is frequently characterized by the narrator as a marriage) should inherit his entire estate including the collection of art objects. This will could easily be circumvented by his relatives since the state would not recognize Schmucke as a legal inheritor. In an effort to thwart the avarice and hypocrisy of his cousins, the Marvilles, and preserve the integrity of the collection, Pons prepared a second will in which the art collection was left to the recently organized state museum, the Louvre. This will is also broken by the family, and the Count Popinot subsequently purchased the entire collection.

A sincere lover of art, Popinot becomes the protector of the authentic values of his society as they are inscribed in its masterworks. He saves the art collection from dispersal by the greedy relatives, and from the instability of the state, as well as the insecurity of the marginalized "foreigner," Schmucke. Balzac's own distrust of the

---

[3] See Pierre-Marc de Biasi, "La Collection Pons comme figure du problématique." De Biasi discusses possible Marxist interpretations with special reference to the work of the important critic Pierre Barbéris who offered a standard Marxist viewpoint in his studies of Balzac's works such as: *Mythes balzaciens* and *Le Monde de Balzac*.

state, in flux since the time of the first Revolution and giving evidence of new instability as he writes in 1847, is revealed in his choice of the rich capitalist, Popinot. Balzac admires his willingness to utilize part of his fortune to benefit the arts, and trusts him to use his power to uphold what he considers to be society's essential values.

The "musée Pons" is, however, only one of the three art collections invoked in and by the novel. Donald Adamson, in his study *The Genesis of* Le Cousin Pons, explains that toward the end of his life in 1846, Balzac himself became an eager art collector (although easily deceived into purchasing fakes). He projects his own rather mediocre collection, transformed by desire and imagination, into the idealized versions of Pons' private museum, and the extraordinary collection of Elie Magus, the art dealer.

Adamson's chapter "Three Art Collections" (119-130) deals thoroughly with the relationships among them, and lists the paintings attributed to each. The inventory of Balzac's own 26 paintings includes the works of Renaissance masters both Italian and Flemish, most of which later proved to be copies. The gallery of Elie Magus (whose name suggests his prophetic, magical wisdom in the world of art) includes among its 100 pictures masterpieces by Giorgione and Balzac's favorite painters, Raphael and Titian.

Magus is presented as a seer of painting whose great gift for intuiting the value of artworks has also become an obsessive passion. He is given mythical status by the narrator, who compares the dealer to an oriental Don Juan and his paintings to beautiful women: "il vivait dans un sérail de beaux tableaux" (5: 210). An immensely rich art dealer, Magus functions in the novel as a successful counterpart to the tragic figure of Pons. Monomaniacal, rival collectors obsessed with perfection in painting, they are important members of Balzac's fictional company of searchers for the absolute found throughout the *Comédie humaine*. Their lives intersect when Magus is asked to evaluate Pons' collection; he finally purchases a few of the best works in the "rape" or theft of the private museum organized by Pons' adversaries.

The "musée Pons" consisted of 67 major paintings constituting a veritable pantheon of "chefs d'oeuvres purs...authentiques" (5: 194). Balzac uses analogies with music to express the beauty of this "concert" of masterworks composed by the two musicians, Pons and his pianist companion, Schmucke. The paintings represent some of the finest artists of the Italian Renaissance and the Northern schools; the French tradition is represented by Claude Lorrain, Chardin, Greuze and only one modern: Géricault.

The four greatest works in the collection (Magus is reduced to tears by their beauty) are Sebastian del Piombo's "Le Chevalier de Malte," Bartolomeo della Porto's "Sainte famille," a portrait by Dürer of the wife of the Holzschuer of Nuremberg, and a landscape by Hobbema. The narrator claims that "l'art humain ne peut aller au delà. C'est supérieur à la nature, qui n'a fait vivre l'original que pendant un moment" (5: 217). Balzac's idealistic aesthetic is clearly expressed in this admiration for the concrete reality of artwork which has the capacity to transcend time and matter, according permanence and value to the ephemeral quality of existence. The collection can perhaps be read as a metaphor for the novel in general, and specifically Balzac's own enterprise, now nearing its completion: the immense effort to represent in fiction the complex dimensions, material and spiritual, of the entire human comedy.

The four masterpieces offer a synthesis of the best in Renaissance art, and symbolize for the narrator its primary virtues: a portrait interesting for its psychological penetration (Dürer), two Italian religious works, and a harmonious Dutch landscape. "Le Chevalier de Malte," included in Balzac's own collection, is compared favorably by the narrator to Piombo's famous portrait of Baccio Bandinelli at the Louvre; its function in the text, however, is undoubtedly symbolic. The aristocratic Knight of Malta, who represented in the popular imagination the virtues of honor, justice and charity, signifies the opposite of the avaricious bourgeoisie who populate the novel.

The painting serves as a recurring symbolic reminder of the lost values of honor and chivalry attributed to the aristocracy. Its companion piece portraying the Holy Family offers the Christian ideal, sadly neglected and undermined, according to the narrator, in contemporary society. The portrait of a German noblewoman and the northern landscape complete this quartet of Renaissance ideal beauty attained by its masters. When Magus contemplates them he is immobilized with admiration and overwhelmed with "le sentiment ineffable que cause la perfection dans l'art" (5: 218).

The narrator concludes this presentation of the "musée Pons" by indicating yet another level of perfection; he names his favorite works at the Louvre: da Vinci's "La Joconde," "L'Antiope" of Correggio and pictures by Raphael and del Sarto, "les plus immenses chefs d'oeuvre de l'art" (218). Balzac's own rather conservative views about art are undoubtedly reflected in this very traditional and generally accepted choice of supreme art works. According to Gautier, in his essays on Balzac in *L'Artiste*, the novelist's taste in painting evolved after 1830 to include Delacroix as well as the Renaissance masters. His first preference had been for the neo-classical artist Anne-Louis Girodet (1767-1824), an academic history painter not much in favor with the romantic generation. What is more important here than Balzac's own views, however, is the prevalent function of painting and sculpture throughout the novel; first as sign or index of character and plot, and then as a symbol of authentic value in a society that is losing its spiritual essence.

At the very moment of his death Pons, the lifelong collector, has a revelation of the truth. He finally understands that everyone except Schmucke is trying to steal his collection, and consequently plans a testament that will preserve it and honor his friend. The narrator compares this supreme moment of intuition to the wisdom of the sculptor who places figures with lighted torches on either side of a tomb in order to illuminate the paths of death. Balzac's narrator analyzes this insight of the artist-sculptor who recognizes that "l'agonie a sa sagesse" (5: 250); apparently the gift of prophecy is often granted to those in the throes of death. The mortuary sculpture of the torches surrounding the tomb illustrates for Balzac's narrator the essentially revelatory function of art; it has the power to valorize life by discovering and uncovering its most profound spiritual and moral significance. Art reveals the truth about human experience just as this mortuary statue suggests and explains Pons' ability to illuminate his past and future for the first time, during his final hours: "La sculpture représente là de grandes idées, elle formule un fait humain" (5: 250).

Balzac's cruel satire of bourgeois customs is fully developed during the scenes of Pons' funeral. The grieving and incompetent Schmucke is totally bewildered and marginalized again by the emphasis on money in all aspects of the degrading experience. He is persuaded by opportunists from the funeral home (la maison Sonet) to purchase an expensive monument to honor and immortalize his friend Pons in the Père Lachaise cemetery.

The mortuary monument would represent three female figures in marble: Music, Painting and Sculpture, "versant des pleurs sur le défunt" (5: 266). This project for a sculpture, however, had originally been intended for the great government minister, De Marsay (an important recurring character in the *Comédie humaine*), but his wife had rejected its design. It had been prepared to illustrate the three glorious days of the July Revolution in 1830 in which De Marsay had played a major role. During the conservative regime of Louis Philippe's "bourgeois" monarchy, the three figures (reminiscent of the classical graces) were transformed into "l'Armée, la Finance et la Famille" (5: 267) for yet another illustrious death, this time a famous bourgeois citizen. For eleven years, the narrator explains, the project had indeed been adapted to all sorts of family situations before being proposed to Schmucke.

A statue designed to serve entirely different circumstances in time and space has indeed become a purely commercial commodity. This replaceable and reusable sculpture signifies the total devalorization and death of art in the dominant bourgeois view of society, in which it has no unique aesthetic value. It becomes a highly effective symbol also of the moral decadence of this class.

The trajectory from the heroic aristocrat, De Marsay, to the pathetic, failed musician Pons, by way of various middle class families whose values were finance and the army, is traced by the floating signifier that the sculptural project has become. This vacant sign traces the decadence of the bourgeoisie from its heroic days of the July Revolution through its hardening into a conservative political hegemony, and finally into a society in which cultural products are only articles with exchange value to serve any profitable occasion. Balzac effectively uses sculpture here to deplore the declining values of the dominant class; the exchangeable mortuary statues symbolize the death of idealism and spirituality as well as the devalorization of art.

Balzac's pessimism concerning human motivation is unmitigated in this final novel in which the satire is often developed to the level of the comic and the grotesque;[4] the expendable mortuary sculp-

---

[4] See Ruth Amossy, "L'Esthétique du grotesque dans *Le Cousin Pons*" in *Balzac et les parents pauvres*.

ture is but one example of the almost hallucinatory quality of his horrific vision of this new world of greed. In addition to the use of art in the text as symbolic of society's changing and degraded values, pictorial comparisons and artistic metaphors are also frequently developed into indices of character and plot.

The first important presence of art in the text is the beautiful fan painted by Watteau that Pons offers to his cousin, the Présidente de Marville. Her disdain of the gift and ignorance of its value, indeed her lack of any knowledge of the artist, are convincing signs of her society's devaluation of art. The narrator's own appreciation of Watteau also suggests that Balzac was slightly in the vanguard of the current reappraisal of eighteenth-century art, fostered by Gautier and later promoted by the Goncourt brothers.

In his recent study of the role of the art collection in *Le Cousin Pons*, Eric Bordas suggests that the Watteau fan is not only a sign of bourgeois incomprehension, but an organizing synecdoche in the novel. This art object represents the excellent quality of the entire collection that it effectively introduces and of which it is a meaningful part.

Pons describes to the Présidente the comic scene of his purchase of the valuable fan from an ignorant dealer in bric-à-brac on the rue de Lappe; the narrator qualifies Pons' lively pantomime as "un modèle digne du pinceau hollandais" (5: 177). Nevertheless, he does not attempt to reproduce in an ekphrastic manner a painting, real or imaginary, suggested by this scene. Instead, typically, he gives the reader, here and throughout the text, the impression that the ephemeral reality presented in fictional language (in this instance Pons' acquisition of the fan) is being filtered through the more concrete, material world of art (a Dutch genre painting), and therefore justified and preserved.

Pons expresses his great joy before the beauty of Watteau's work in exclamatory style; he compares the brush strokes to a writing flourish that suggests the unity of word and image: "Quelle verve! quel coloris! Et c'est fait! tout d'un trait! comme un paraphe de maître d'écriture; on ne sent plus le travail! Et de l'autre côté, tenez: un bal dans un salon! C'est l'hiver et l'été!...Vous voyez, la virole est en or, et elle est terminée de chaque côté par un tout petit rubis que j'ai décrassé!" (5: 177-78). The narrator, however, does not choose to describe the fan in detail nor attempt to transpose its qualities in linguistic terms.

This rather curious lack of ekphrastic representation in the text, given the great number of allusions to art, and Balzac's practice of artistic transposition in many other texts (e.g., *Le Chef d'oeuvre inconnu*, *La Fille aux yeux d'or*), is compensated by the recurring use of pictorial comparisons. The generous forms of the concierge Cibot, for example, are compared to those of a Rubens female figure; the frightening Madame Sauvage's name is seconded by the analogy made with a painting by the Dutch painter, Adrien Brauwer, entitled "Witches leaving for the Sabbath." The unscrupulous lawyer, Fraisier, is characterized as a serpent and a painted devil: "Fraisier, calme, froid comme un serpent qui se serait dressé sur sa queue, allongeait sa tête plate et se tenait dans la pose que les peintres prêtent à Méphistophélès" (5: 244).

In Pons' second will he ironically leaves his Goya drawing of a monkey's head to the uncultured Président Camusot. Significantly, suggesting his own martyrdom, he donates his sketch by Rubens for the famous painting, "The Descent of the Cross," to his church parish. These examples among many suffice to illustrate that painting as sign in the text serves as index to character and plot, but also valorizes experience and accords a permanent spiritual dimension to ordinary human situations.

Perhaps the best illustration of this function of painting in the text occurs during Pons' prolonged agony. Already near death, he collapses at the sight of the empty spaces on his walls, silent witnesses to the treachery and thievery of those around him. His trustworthy partner, the childlike and almost grotesque musician Schmucke, literally restores him to life through his devoted friendship; he felt "des jouissances presque égales à celles de l'amour" (5: 246) as he administered aid to Pons.

The relationship between Pons and Schmucke is elevated to a quasi-religious level through art. Idealized in suffering, they are compared to a Renaissance Pietà in which Schmucke, like a mother, breathes life into his dying friend. Their friendship is valorized by this artistic metaphor, representing a love nourished in suffering: "Il baisa son ami sur les yeux comme ses *Marie* que les grands sculpteurs italiens ont sculptées dans leurs bas-reliefs appelés *Pietà*, baisant le Christ. Ces efforts divins, cette effusion d'une vie dans une autre, cette oeuvre de mère et d'amante fut couronnée d'un plein succès" (5: 245). Pons, revived, reacts to this extraordinary proof of friendship in a kind of epiphany: "Pons comprit alors à quel saint dévouement, à quelle puissance d'amitié cette résurrection était due" (5: 246).

In Balzac's final novel, art alone seems to authenticate human experience and hold the promise of preserving its essential values. In spite of the prevailing pessimism about human desire and motivation, the friendship of the two musicians, who have been mocked and destroyed, transcends the cruel limits of the society that defines them. The art collection also succeeds in surmounting these constraints, although it has been mutilated; its beauty and significance will be preserved as evidence of civilization's highest achievement.

Balzac's narrator develops a Baudelairean triple correspondence among the arts (music, painting and poetry) to express Schmucke's talent at the piano, and to suggest the essential unity of artistic expression beyond the apparent differences in each medium. In a scene that typifies and symbolizes the situation of the arts during the July Monarchy, the German musician plays an extraordinary concert in the middle of the night to console his sick friend. He played with the "perfection raphaélesque de Chopin" (5: 253), and the Dante-like fire of Lizst; in a moment of inspiration he became both Beethoven and Paganini (creator and interpreter). While the annoyed bourgeois neighbors hear only cacophony, Pons is enchanted by the sublime music produced by his friend which the narrator calls poetry: "Il [Schmucke] se surpassa, et plongea le vieux musicien qui l'écoutait dans l'extase que Raphael a peinte, et qu'on va voir à Bologne" (5: 254).

The divinely inspired piano music evokes not only the poetry of Dante but also the paintings of Saint Cecilia and her musicians exécutés by Raphael. The German romantic musician, a naive outsider to this society that scorns him, also achieves transcendence through art: "L'exécution, arrivée à ce degré de perfection, met en apparence l'exécutant à la hauteur du poète, il est au compositeur ce que l'acteur est à l'auteur, un divin traducteur de choses divines" (5: 253).

The bleak portrait of human greed and meanness offered by *Le Cousin Pons* is, finally, curiously tempered by Balzac's faith in the authenticity of art and friendship. Art is seen to reveal and preserve the deepest meanings and values of life, and only friendship, in the order of human relationships, seems to escape the financial, material constraints of marriage and family in this patriarchal society portrayed as degraded by money and power.

Conclusion

LOUIS BOULANGER, PAINTER-POET OF ROMANTICISM –FROM MAZEPPA TO PETRARCH

THE writers of the romantic generation in France were profoundly interested in the variety of possible interrelations between the arts. Before Baudelaire expressed his theories about the basic unity of sensory experience, and its expression in the correspondence between the arts, the romantic writers, painters and musicians were practicing various forms of ekphrasis and transposition. The first viewing of Boulanger's painting "Le Triomphe de Pétrarque," commissioned by the famous Marquis de Custine in 1836, was attended by a roster of celebrated romantics. Chopin played a new Nocturne, and Théophile Gautier read his poem based on the immense painting that presented an idealized version of the artist and his function. Poetry, music and painting were thus united and celebrated in a veritable happening; it symbolized romantic aspirations for collaboration among artists, and promoted the creation of art forms to be made richer from the development of interartistic relations.

This highly symbolic romantic event represents the summit of Boulanger's career as the interpreter of romantic literature and the creator of romantic iconography. As an artist he is unfortunately neglected today, and in his own time was severely criticized by Baudelaire, especially in his discussions of the paintings in the Salon of 1845. Baudelaire's negative comments are, however, enlightening; he considers that Boulanger diminished his talent by painting in the shadow of his great friend, Victor Hugo. According to Baudelaire he permitted poetry to dominate his painting (he was an important illustrator of Hugo's works); the great success of "Le Supplice de

Mazeppa" (1827) apparently ruined Boulanger's potential to be other than a strictly literary painter or illustrator.

This judgment reflects an anti-romantic bias on the part of Baudelaire, and was corrected by various critics after the Salon of 1859 who praised Boulanger as a significant interpreter of romantic literature, and actually ranked him with Delacroix as the major painters of French Romanticism.

Although most critics agree that Boulanger's portraits of romantic writers, and especially Hugo and his family, are probably his finest work, his major successes were the painting "Mazeppa" in the Salon of 1827 (now in Rouen's Musée des Beaux-Arts), and "Le Triomphe de Pétrarque" from the Salon of 1836. In my view, the two paintings mark symbolically the development of the romantic concept of the artist–from the suffering, misunderstood genius, as exemplified in the legend of Mazeppa, to the glorified concept of the poet-philosopher, like Petrarch a spiritual, intellectual guide for society.

Although it is true that Boulanger was primarily a literary painter who illustrated romantic poetry and fiction, his paintings of Mazeppa and Petrarch inspired both Hugo and Gautier to write important poems that interpret them. "Le Supplice de Mazeppa," considered one of the major new romantic works after the Salon exhibit of 1827, was based on Byron's poem about the Ukrainian nobleman who was punished for seducing the wife of the ruler. He was tied to a wild horse and taken for a mad and dangerous ride through the countryside, until he was finally rescued by the peasants who were later to become his subjects. Hugo transforms this legend of Mazeppa, taken from Byron's poem and Boulanger's painting, as well as Voltaire's history, into a romantic allegory of genius. The French artists did not know Pushkin's famous poem on the same subject.

> Ainsi, lorsqu'un mortel, sur qui son dieu s'étale,
> S'est vu lier vivant sur ta croupe fatale,
>   Génie, ardent coursier,
> En vain il lutte, hélas! tu bondis, tu l'emportes
> Hors du monde réel, dont tu brises les portes
>   Avec tes pieds d'acier!
>
>   (Pléiade 1: 674, 17-22)

The wild horse thus symbolizes the uncontrollable force of genius that leads the artist to unknown regions of knowledge and experience. Hugo's poem is not really ekphrastic since he does not attempt to reproduce elements of the image other than the horse and its rider. Boulanger's first treatment of the subject (several versions were done later) dealt only with the scene of departure and was entitled "Le Départ." Hugo's poem narrates the wild ride in detail, suggesting its furious movement through rhythm and stanzaic arrangement. His quality as a very visual poet is also quite marked in this poem, although the color scheme is limited to familiar, symbolic contrasts between darkness and light. Hugo also addressed and dedicated a series of important poems to his friend, Boulanger, in at least four later collections of poetry, but did not interpret or transpose any other works of the painter.

Boulanger, on the other hand, illustrated a series of poems from Hugo's *Odes et Ballades* and *Orientales* in ekphrastic paintings and lithographs which perhaps exhibit his most interesting and unusual work (e.g. "Les Djinns," "La Ronde du Sabbat" and "Le Feu du ciel"). These pictures correspond to the romantic fascination with the fantastic, including scenes of terror and dynamic images of the supernatural. His originality as an artist indeed lies in these illustrations. According to his principal biographer, Aristide Marie,[1] he is above all the painter of phantoms and demons. Strongly influenced by Goya and the poetry of his great friend, Hugo, he is perhaps the most fervent illustrator of the romantic imagination in its early fantastic or "frenetic" phase.

Gautier's poem, "Le Triomphe de Pétrarque," discussed in detail in Chapter 1, is based on the second major success in Boulanger's career. In this widely praised painting (Salon of 1836), Boulanger chose a universal symbol to glorify poetry, and reduced the accessory details to produce a rather traditional and static, even neo-classical work. It is indeed much closer in technique and composition to Ingres than to Delacroix whom he so greatly admired. Instead of the suffering and isolated genius figure Mazeppa, he offers the portrait of a great artist adulated by the public. This paint-

---

[1] Marie's *Le Peintre-poète Louis Boulanger* remains the most complete and invaluable survey of Boulanger's work; it contains many illustrations of the paintings and drawings that are not reproduced elsewhere.

ing undoubtedly represents the projection of a forceful wish and desire on the part of the painter; his biographers suggest that he was very conscious of being a "raté" or failure, and that he consequently suffered prolonged periods of doubt and depression. Although he was a close friend of the major romantic writers including Sainte-Beuve and Pétrus Borel, he never attained their level of success. The only verses ever published by Boulanger, dedicated to his friend Sainte-Beuve, reveal a very romantic sense of disillusionment, an incapacity to realize his potential and achieve his aspirations.

> Non, je ne reçus point d'en-haut ce don céleste
> Qui fait, lorsque tout meurt et s'efface, que reste
> Debout, l'oeuvre immortelle et que dans l'avenir,
> La gloire de l'auteur resplendit aussi belle
> Qu'aux grands jours où la ville en fête solennelle
> Promenait ses tableaux que l'on allait bénir!
> Pourtant ces Florentins, ces élus du Génie,
> Que ta muse à mes yeux présente pleins de vie,
> Souvent de leur lumière ils viennent m'inonder,
> Et quelquefois hélas! aux élans de mon âme,
> J'ai cru, pauvre insensé, qu'un rayon de la flamme,
> Pénétrant dans mon ombre, allait la féconder.[2]

In this elegiac poem of 1836, Boulanger offers a kind of personal commentary on his own painting of Petrarch's triumph. He stresses the importance of Italian Renaissance art, whose techniques he and other romantic artists tried to emulate, in their attempt to renew the restrictive neo-classical tradition inherited from David and perpetuated by Ingres. He was particularly moved by the great Florentine artists whose special light and use of rich color inspired his best mythological and historical paintings, including "Le Triomphe de Pétrarque." He is, however, painfully aware that his aspiration often exceeded his talent, that the brilliant light of Renaissance painting did not sufficiently penetrate his personal darkness. The central scene he describes in this poem of the solemn festival, during which the city of Florence celebrates its artists by having their paintings blessed, suggests the stately procession of Petrarch followed by a serious and adoring public in Boulanger's own painting.

---

[2] This poem is presented by Marie, *Louis Boulanger*, p. 45.

Boulanger never repeated the great success of this portrait of the artist, idealized and appreciated, that resumes the aspirations of the romantic generation in 1836. It celebrates their great love of Renaissance art and the power of creativity, in effect a renewed confidence in the artist's role as intellectual and spiritual guide of the people. After the Revolution of 1830 and before the collapse of Romantic idealism in the failure of the Revolution of 1848, it reflects a new philosophy of the inevitability of material and spiritual progress, celebrated by Michelet in his histories, and exemplified in the social conscience of writers like Hugo and Sand.

In the Salon of 1859 Boulanger successfully exhibited 14 paintings with literary themes, and he became the Director of the Ecole des Beaux-Arts in Dijon in 1860. His career therefore spans the Romantic period, and even though he suffered from incomprehension, his work represents perhaps better than any other painter's the romantic fascination with interarts relations. Before Gautier developed his practice of "transposition d'art," Boulanger illustrated Hugo's early fantasy poems of exotic and oriental imagery. His fine portraits of Balzac, Sand, Hugo and others capture the unusual energy and beauty of the great artists of his generation. The series of Mazeppa paintings he executed corresponded to a profound need in the romantic psyche to express in visual images the torments of the creative person; Géricault, Delacroix, Vernet and Chassériau all painted similar scenes of the mad ride of genius based on the same literary models. His love of Petrarch and Renaissance art is echoed in George Sand's idealized portrait of the sixteenth-century Venitian mosaic makers. This admiration is finally codified and institutionalized in Balzac's choice of supreme paintings for Pons's private museum. His collection of masterpieces featuring important Renaissance paintings remarkably resists appropriation by the avaricious bourgeois, and continues to symbolize authentic values in post-revolutionary society.

WORKS CITED

Adamson, Donald. *The Genesis of* Le Cousin Pons. Oxford: Oxford UP, 1966.
Amossy, Ruth. "L'Esthétique du grotesque dans *Le Cousin Pons.*" *Balzac et les parents pauvres*. Ed. Françoise van Rossum-Guyon and Michiel van Brederode. Paris: CDU and SEDES, 1981.
Balzac, Honoré de. *Le Cousin Pons*. Vol. 5. *La Comédie humaine*. 7 vols. Paris: Seuil (L'Intégrale), 1966.
———. *La Fille aux yeux d'or*. Vol. 5. *La Comédie humaine*. Ed. Pierre-Georges Castex. 12 vols. Paris: Gallimard (Pléiade), 1976-81.
———. *La Peau de chagrin*. Vol. 6. *La Comédie humaine*. 7 vols. Paris: Seuil (L'Intégrale), 1966.
Barrère, Jean-Bertrand. *La Fantaisie de Victor Hugo*. 3 vols. Paris: Corti, 1949.
———. "Victor Hugo et les arts plastiques." *Revue de littérature comparée* 30 (1956): 180-208.
Baudelaire, Charles. *Fleurs du mal*. Paris: Garnier-Flammarion, 1964.
Baudrillard, Jean. *Simulations*. Trans. Paul Foss, Paul Patton, and Philip Beitchman. New York: Columbia UP, Semiotext(e), 1983.
Bénichou, Paul. *Le Sacre de l'écrivain 1750-1830*. Paris: Corti, 1973.
Biasi, Pierre-Marc de. "La Collection Pons comme figure du problématique." *Balzac et les Parents pauvres*. Ed. Françoise van Rossum-Guyon and Michiel van Brederode. Paris: CDU and SEDES, 1981.
Bonard, Olivier. *La Peinture dans la création balzacienne: Invention et vision picturales de* La Maison du Chat-qui-pelote *au* Père Goriot. Geneva: Droz, 1969.
Bordas, Eric. "Le Rôle de la peinture dans *Le Cousin Pons.*" *Australian Journal of French Studies* 32.1 (1995): 19-37.
Bourget, Jean-Loup. "Balzac et le pictural." *Romanic Review* 64.4 (1973): 286-295.
Brombert, Victor. *La Prison romantique*. Paris: Corti, 1975.
Chambers, Ross. *Mélancolie et opposition: les débuts du modernisme en France*. Paris: Corti, 1987.
———. "Gautier et le complexe de Pygmalion." *Revue d'histoire littéraire de la France* 72.4 (1972): 641-658.
Clements, Robert J. "Dürer's *Knight, Death and the Devil*: Five Literary Readings." CRCL/RCLC (Winter 1979): 1-8.
Felman, Shoshanna. "Rereading Femininity." *Yale French Studies* 62 (1981): 19-44.
Frappier-Mazur, Lucienne. "Nostalgie, dédoublement, et écriture dans *Histoire de ma vie.*" NCFS 17.3-4 (1989): 265-275.

Gautier, Théophile. *Poésies complètes*. 3 vols. Ed. René Jasinski. Paris: Nizet, 1970.
———. *Emaux et camées*. Ed. Madeleine Cottin. Paris: Minard, 1973.
———. *España*. Ed. René Jasinski. Paris: Vuibert, 1929.
Greene, John P. "Balzac's Most Helpless Heroine: The Art Collection in *Le Cousin Pons*." *French Review* 16.1 (October 1995): 13-23.
Heffernan, James A. W. *Museum of Words: The Poetics of Ekphrasis from Homer to Ashberry*. Chicago: U of Chicago P, 1993.
Hirschell, Georges. *Balzac und Delacroix, Streiflecter auf den Roman*, La Fille aux yeux d'or. Bâle: University of Bâle, 1946.
Hugo, Victor. *Oeuvres poétiques*. 2 vols. Paris: Gallimard, 1967.
———. *Toute la lyre. Poésies*. 3 vols. Paris: Seuil, 1972.
Kelley, David. "Gautier et Baudelaire." *Baudelaire, Mallarmé, Valéry: New Essays in Honor of Lloyd Austin*. Ed. Malcolm Bowie et al. Cambridge: Cambridge UP, 1982.
———. "Transpositions." *Artistic Relations: Literature and The Visual Arts in Nineteenth-Century France*. Ed. Peter Collier and Robert Lethbridge. New Haven: Yale UP, 1994.
Kenaan-Kedar, Nurith. "The Ekphrastic Components of Victor Hugo's *Notre-Dame de Paris*." *Pictures into Words: Theoretical and Descriptive Approaches to Ekphrasis*. Ed. Valerie Robillard and Els Jongeneel. Amsterdam: V.U. UP, 1998.
Krieger, Murray. *Ekphrasis: The Illusion of the Natural Sign*. Baltimore: Johns Hopkins UP, 1991.
Kristeva, Julia. *Soleil noir, dépression et mélancolie*. Paris: Gallimard, 1987.
Kuhn, Reinhard. *The Demon of Noontide: Ennui in Western Literature*. Princeton: Princeton UP, 1976.
L'Hôpital, Madeleine. *La Notion d'artiste chez George Sand*. Paris: Boivin, 1946.
Lipschutz, Ilse H. *Spanish Painting and the French Romantics*. Cambridge, Mass.: Harvard UP, 1972.
———. "Théophile Gautier, le musée espagnol et Zurbarán." *T. Gautier, L'art et l'artiste: Actes du colloque international*. 2 vols. Montpellier: U Paul Valéry, 1982.
Lucey, Michael. "Balzac's Queer Cousins and Their Friends." *Queer Readings in Fiction*. Ed. Eve K. Sedgwick. Durham, NC: Duke UP, 1997.
Majewski, Henry F. *Paradigm and Parody: Images of Creativity in French Romanticism*. Charlottesville, Virginia: U Virginia P, 1989.
Maleuvre, Didier. *Museum Memories, History, Technology, Art*. Stanford: Stanford UP, 1999.
Marie, Aristide. *Le Peintre-poète Louis Boulanger*. Paris: H. Floury, 1925.
Meyer, Jeffrey. *Painting and the Novel*. Manchester: Manchester UP, 1975.
Michelet, Jules. *Histoire de France*. 16 vols. Ed. Claude Mettra. Lausanne: Rencontre, 1965-67.
Miller, Nancy K. "Arachnologies: The Woman, the Text and the Critic." *Subject to Change*. New York: Columbia UP, 1986.
Miquel, Pierre. "T. Gautier et les paysagistes." *T. Gautier, l'art et l'artiste: Colloque international*. 2 vols. Montpellier: U Paul Valéry, 1982.
Mitchell, W. J. Thomas. *Iconology: Image, Text, Ideology*. Chicago: U of Chicago P, 1986.
Montandon, Alain. "Ecritures de l'image chez Théophile Gautier." In *Icons-Texts-Iconotexts*. Ed. Peter Wagner. European Cultures: Studies in Literature and the Arts 6. Berlin, New York: Walter de Gruyter, 1996.
Naginski, Isabelle Hoog. *George Sand: Writing for Her Life*. New Brunswick: Rutgers UP, 1991.

Nash, Susanne. *Les Contemplations of Victor Hugo: An Allegory of the Creative Process*. Princeton: Princeton UP, 1977.
Nerval, Gérard de. *Oeuvres*. 2 vols. Paris: Garnier, 1958.
Panofsky, Erwin. *The Life and Art of Albrecht Dürer*. Princeton: Princeton UP, 1955.
Pantazzi, Michael. "The Greatest Landscape Painter of Our Time." *Corot*. Gary Tinterow, Michael Pantazzi, and Vincent Pomarède. New York: The Metropolitan Museum of Art, 1996.
Patty, James S. *Dürer in French Letters*. Paris-Geneva: Champion-Slatkine, 1989.
Poli, Annarosa. *L'Italie dans la vie et l'oeuvre de George Sand*. Paris: Armand Colin, 1960.
Porter, Laurence M. "Mourning and Melancholia in Nerval's *Aurélia*." *Studies in Romanticism* 15.2 (1976): 289-306.
Rambeau, Marie-Paule. *Chopin dans la vie et l'oeuvre de George Sand*. Paris: Les Belles lettres, 1985.
Riffaterre, Michael. *Semiotics of Poetry*. Bloomington and London: Indiana UP, 1987.
Robaut, Alfred. *L'Oeuvre de Corot: catalogue raisonné et illustré*. Paris: L. Laget, 1905. Reprinted Paris, 1965.
Sand, George. *Correspondance générale*. Paris: Calman-Lévy, 1878.
———. *Histoire de ma vie* (1854). *Oeuvres autobiographiques*. 2 vols. Ed. George Lupin. Paris: Gallimard (Pléiade), 1970.
———. *Les Maîtres mosaïstes*. Paris: Michel Lévy, 1869.
———. *Les Maîtres mosaïstes*. Ed. Annarosa Poli. Florence: Sansoni, 1966.
———. *Les Maîtres mosaïstes*. Ed. Marie-Madeleine Fragonard. *Vies d'artistes*. Paris: Presses de la Cité, 1992.
———. *Questions d'art et de littérature*. Paris: Calman-Lévy, 1878.
Schick, Constance G. *Seductive Resistance: The Poetry of Théophile Gautier*. Amsterdam-Atlanta, GA: Rodopi, 1994.
Schiesari, Juliana. *The Gendering of Melancholia: Feminism, Psychoanalysis, and the Symbolics of Loss in Renaissance Literature*. Ithaca and London: Cornell UP, 1992.
Schor, Naomi. *George Sand and Idealism*. New York: Columbia UP, 1993.
Scott, David. *Pictorialist Poetics: Poetry and the Visual Arts in Nineteenth-Century France*. Cambridge: Cambridge UP, 1988.
Spector, Jack J. *Delacroix: The Death of Sardanapalus*. New York: Viking P, 1974.
Steiner, Wendy. *The Colors of Rhetoric: Problems in the Relation between Modern Literature and Painting*. Chicago: U of Chicago P, 1982.
Thompson, C. W. *Victor Hugo and the Graphic Arts (1820-33)*. Geneva: Droz, 1970.
Vigny, Alfred de. *Oeuvres complètes*. 2 vols. Paris: Gallimard (Pléiade), 1948.
Voisin, Marcel. *Le soleil et la nuit: l'imaginaire dans l'oeuvre de T. Gautier*. Brussels: Brussels UP, 1981.

ILLUSTRATIONS

Francisco de Zurbarán, "The Ecstasy of Saint Francis," 1664. Alte Pinakothek, Munich

114 TRANSPOSING ART INTO TEXTS

Jean-Baptiste-Camille Corot, "Landscape with Lake and Boatman," 1839. The J. Paul Getty Museum

Albrecht Dürer, "The Knight, Death and the Devil," Engraving, 1513. The Metropolitan Museum of Art, New York. Harris Brisbane Dick Fund

Albrecht Dürer, "Melencolia I," Engraving, 1514. The Metropolitan Museum of Art, New York. Fletcher Fund, 1919

"St. Mark in Ecstasy," 1545. St. Mark's Basilica, Venice. Designed by Titian and executed by the Zuccato workshop

Eugène Delacroix, "Wild Horse" (Cheval sauvage), Lithograph. 1828.
The Metropolitan Museum of Art, New York

ILLUSTRATIONS 119

Eugène Delacroix, "Horse attacked by a Tiger" (Cheval terrassé par un tigre), Lithograph. 1828. The Metropolitan Museum of Art, New York. Rogers Fund, 1922

Eugène Delacroix, "La Mort de Sardanapale," 1827. Louvre Museum

ILLUSTRATIONS 121

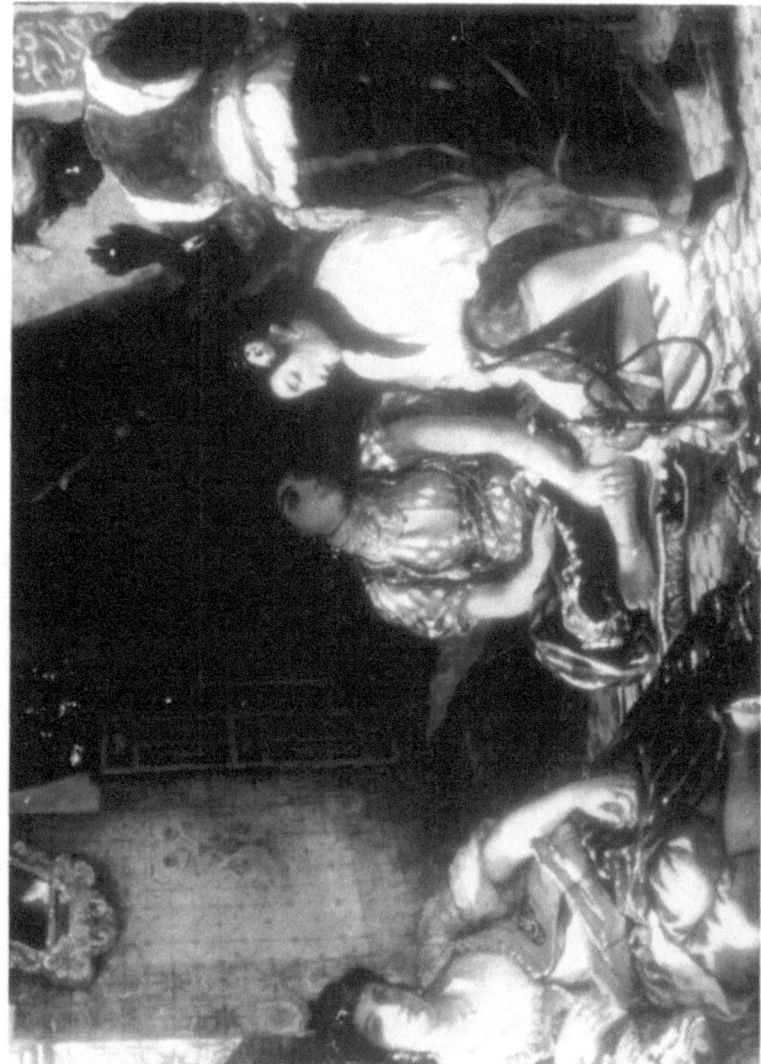

Eugène Delacroix, "Femmes d'Alger dans leur appartement," 1834. Louvre Museum

Louis Boulanger, "Le Triomphe de Pétrarque," 1836. Private collection

Louis Boulanger, "Victor Hugo," 1832. La Maison de Victor Hugo, Paris

Louis Boulanger, "George Sand," 1837. Private collection

Louis Boulanger, "Portrait de Balzac en robe de chambre," 1836.
Musée des Beaux-Arts, Tours

NORTH CAROLINA STUDIES IN THE ROMANCE LANGUAGES AND LITERATURES

I.S.B.N. Prefix 0-8078-

Recent Titles

EL TIEMPO Y LOS MÁRGENES. EUROPA COMO UTOPÍA Y COMO AMENAZA EN LA LITERATURA ESPAÑOLA, por Jesús Torrecilla. 1996. (No. 253). *-9257-2.*
THE AESTHETICS OF ARTIFICE: VILLIERS'S *L'EVE FUTURE*, by Marie Lathers. 1996. (No. 254). *-9254-8.*
DISLOCATIONS OF DESIRE: GENDER, IDENTITY, AND STRATEGY IN *LA REGENTA*, by Alison Sinclair. 1998. (No. 255). *-9259-9.*
THE POETICS OF INCONSTANCY, ETIENNE DURAND AND THE END OF RENAISSANCE VERSE, by Hoyt Rogers. 1998. (No. 256). *-9260-2.*
RONSARD'S CONTENTIOUS SISTERS: THE PARAGONE BETWEEN POETRY AND PAINTING IN THE WORKS OF PIERRE DE RONSARD, by Roberto E. Campo. 1998. (No. 257). *-9261-0.*
THE RAVISHMENT OF PERSEPHONE: EPISTOLARY LYRIC IN THE *SIÈCLE DES LUMIÈRES*, by Julia K. De Pree. 1998. (No. 258). *-9262-9.*
CONVERTING FICTION: COUNTER REFORMATIONAL CLOSURE IN THE SECULAR LITERATURE OF GOLDEN AGE SPAIN, by David H. Darst. 1998. (No. 259). *-9263-7.*
GALDÓS'S *SEGUNDA MANERA*: RHETORICAL STRATEGIES AND AFFECTIVE RESPONSE, by Linda M. Willem. 1998. (No. 260). *-9264-5.*
A MEDIEVAL PILGRIM'S COMPANION. REASSESSING *EL LIBRO DE LOS HUÉSPEDES* (ESCORIAL MS. h.I.13), by Thomas D. Spaccarelli. 1998. (No. 261). *-9265-3.*
'PUEBLOS ENFERMOS': THE DISCOURSE OF ILLNESS IN THE TURN-OF-THE-CENTURY SPANISH AND LATIN AMERICAN ESSAY, by Michael Aronna. 1999. (No. 262). *-9266-1.*
RESONANT THEMES. LITERATURE, HISTORY, AND THE ARTS IN NINETEENTH- AND TWENTIETH-CENTURY EUROPE. ESSAYS IN HONOR OF VICTOR BROMBERT, by Stirling Haig. 1999. (No. 263). *-9267-X.*
RAZA, GÉNERO E HIBRIDEZ EN *EL LAZARILLO DE CIEGOS CAMINANTES*, por Mariselle Meléndez. 1999. (No. 264). *-9268-8.*
DEL ESCENARIO A LA PANTALLA: LA ADAPTACIÓN CINEMATOGRÁFICA DEL TEATRO ESPAÑOL, por María Asunción Gómez. 2000. (No. 265). *-9269-6.*
THE LEPER IN BLUE: COERCIVE PERFORMANCE AND THE CONTEMPORARY LATIN AMERICAN THEATER, by Amalia Gladhart. 2000. (No. 266). *-9270-X.*
THE CHARM OF CATASTROPHE: A STUDY OF RABELAIS'S *QUART LIVRE*, by Alice Fiola Berry. 2000. (No. 267). *-9271-8.*
PUERTO RICAN CULTURAL IDENTITY AND THE WORK OF LUIS RAFAEL SÁNCHEZ, by John Dimitri Perivolaris. 2000. (No. 268). *-9272-6.*
MANNERISM AND BAROQUE IN SEVENTEENTH-CENTURY FRENCH POETRY: THE EXAMPLE OF TRISTAN L'HERMITE, by James Crenshaw Shepard. 2001. (No. 269). *-9273-4.*
RECLAIMING THE BODY: MARÍA DE ZAYA'S EARLY MODERN FEMINISM, by Lisa Vollendorf. 2001. (No. 270). *-9274-2.*
FORGED GENEALOGIES: SAINT-JOHN PERSE'S CONVERSATIONS WITH CULTURE, by Carol Rigolot. 2001. (No. 271). *-9275-0.*
VISIONES DE ESTEREOSCOPIO (PARADIGMA DE HIBRIDACIÓN EN EL ARTE Y LA NARRATIVA DE LA VANGUARDIA ESPAÑOLA), por María Soledad Fernández Utrera. 2001. (No. 272). *-9276-9.*
TRANSPOSING ART INTO TEXTS IN FRENCH ROMANTIC LITERATURE, by Henry F. Majewski. 2002. (No. 273). *-9277-7.*

When ordering please cite the *ISBN Prefix* plus the last four digits for each title.

Send orders to: University of North Carolina Press
P.O. Box 2288
CB# 6215
Chapel Hill, NC 27515-2288
U.S.A.

www.ingramcontent.com/pod-product-compliance
Lightning Source LLC
Chambersburg PA
CBHW020750230426
43665CB00009B/557